The Metaphysical Foundations of Love

THOMISTIC RESSOURCEMENT SERIES

Volume 10

SERIES EDITORS

Matthew Levering, *Mundelein Seminary*

Thomas Joseph White, OP, *Dominican House of Studies*

EDITORIAL BOARD

Serge-Thomas Bonino, OP, *Pontifical University of St. Thomas Aquinas*

Gilles Emery, OP, *University of Fribourg (Switzerland)*

Reinhard Hütter, *The Catholic University of America*

Bruce Marshall, *Southern Methodist University*

Emmanuel Perrier, OP, *Dominican Studium, Toulouse*

Richard Schenk, OP, *University of Freiburg (Germany)*

Kevin White, *The Catholic University of America*

The Metaphysical Foundations of Love

Aquinas on Participation, Unity, and Union

ANTHONY T. FLOOD

The Catholic University of America Press
Washington, D.C.

For Dorothy, Cecilia, Simon, and Hugh

Copyright © 2018
The Catholic University of America Press
All rights reserved
The paper used in this publication meets the minimum
requirements of American National Standards for Information
Science—Permanence of Paper for Printed Library Materials,
ANSI Z39.48-1984.

Cataloging-in-Publication Data available
from the Library of Congress
ISBN 978-0-8132-3120-4

Contents

Acknowledgments   vii
Introduction   ix

1. **Love as a Unitive Force**   1
   Union and Friendship   1
   Unity and the Love of Self   11
   From Unity to Union   18

2. **Degrees of Union**   25
   Distinctions Pertaining to the Unions of Similitude and Possession   25
   The Equalizing Effect of Charity   32
   Marriage as the Greatest Human Union   35

3. **Participation and the Love of God**   44
   The Love of Self and the Love of God   44
   The Natural Inclination to the Love of God   50
   The Supernatural Love of God   56

4. **Conformity and Sin**   67
   The Necessity of Conformity   67
   Sin and Hatred   71
   Satan and Temptation   80

Contents

5. **The Fulfillment of Love in God** — 85
   Love and Self-Governance 85
   Love and Worship 91
   Love and Obedience to the Divine Will 97

6. **The Love of Self and Subjectivity** — 110
   The Love of Self and Conscious Self-Experience 110
   Participation, Irreducibility, and Omnisubjectivity 120
   Subjectivity in Light of Charity 127

Conclusion — 134

Bibliography — 139

Index — 145

Acknowledgments

As a continuation of my research program, I will begin by acknowledging previous reviewers of my first book and articles on the considered themes in Aquinas. Two journals deserve special mention, as I have revised articles they published to form chapters in this work. Chapter 3, section 1 ("The Love of Self and the Love of God") revisits and significantly revises an argument I first made in "Aquinas on Self-Love and Love of God: The Foundations for and Perfection of Subjectivity," *International Philosophical Quarterly* 56, no. 1 (March 2016): 45–55.

Chapter 3, section 2 ("The Natural Inclination to the Love of God") revisits and significantly revises an argument I first made in "Marriage as Friendship: Aquinas's View in Light of His Account of Self-Love," *Nova et Vetera* 13, no. 2 (2015): 441–58. I thank both journals for the permission to reuse these sections.

Specific to this project, I wish to thank the reviewers for their helpful comments. I thank Aldene Fredenburg and Theresa B. Walker for their editorial assistance. In addition, William Mahoney deserves special mention for his assistance with both editing and argumentation. I am grateful to John B. Martino for shepherding my proposal and manuscript through the review process. Lastly, I thank my wife, Dorothy, for putting up with the research and writing process (and with me).

Introduction

St. Thomas Aquinas identifies love as the source and summit of the life of each human being. Everything in the created realm issues forth from God's creative love, and the ultimate end of all human persons is the greatest possible union with God. Aquinas contends that the love of friendship allows for the greatest union between two persons; thus, the greatest union with God takes the form of friendship. He identifies the virtue of charity as precisely this union of friendship with God—imperfect in this life but fully realized in the life to come.

In addition to the grand metaphysical bookends of human existence, love also serves as the structuring notion of Aquinas's practical philosophy. He characterizes much of human life in terms of three basic love relations: the love a person has for God, or simply the love of God; love of self; and love of neighbor. Love of self derives from personal substantial unity. It is logically prior to love of neighbor and serves as a template for the latter. If a person loves himself rightly, he will love others rightly. On the other hand, if he relates to himself through a disordered love, he neither can relate to others rightly nor enter into a deep union with them. Moreover, due to a person's metaphysical participation in God, a person loves himself properly only when he loves God more than himself. Thus, failing to love God appropriately entails an inability to relate to others with a fully developed love. Conversely, the love of God positions a person to relate to others with an authentic love and enter into the union of friendship with them.

In my previous book, *The Root of Friendship*, I made the case that the notion of subjectivity, understood as each person's ongoing self-experience, forms a central element to Aquinas's anthropology.[1] My basic argument was that, since friendship derives from the love of self, anything relevant about friendship can be affirmed of self-love. Since friendship, though initially constituted principally by the will, involves the experience of the beloved's interior life, so self-love, while also initiated by the will, involves an experience of one's own self. Moreover, as self-love is based on the metaphysically deeper basis of unity versus union, the self-experience generated by self-love must be a more permanent and continual self-experience relative to the experience of the other in friendship. While I am no longer entirely satisfied with all the details of the argument in *The Root of Friendship*, I still affirm the basic structure and conclusion. I revisit and revise this argument in the final chapter of this work, but the topic of subjectivity is not the main focus of this book.

In articles written after the previous book was published, I developed various aspects of the argument for Thomistic subjectivity, particularly in terms of the underlying connections of participation, unity, and union.[2] I concluded that a book treating Aquinas's account of these notions and how they affect his understanding of love would be valuable. I hope this book adequately accomplishes this. I wrote the first five chapters to be independent of my argument for Thomistic subjectivity so that, if the reader rejects the latter, he or she might still find the former valuable. However, since I think my argument for subjectivity naturally follows upon the considerations on love, the last chapter offers my revised, full argument for Thom-

---

1. Anthony T. Flood, *The Root of Friendship: Self-Love and Self-Governance in Aquinas* (Washington, D.C.: The Catholic University of America Press, 2014).

2. Flood, "Marriage as Friendship: Aquinas's View in Light of His Account of Self-Love," *Nova et Vetera* 13, no. 2 (2015): 441–58, and "Aquinas on Self-Love and Love of God: The Foundations for and Perfection of Subjectivity," *International Philosophical Quarterly* 56, no. 1 (March 2016): 45–55.

istic subjectivity in light of the analyses of the previous chapters.

In terms of the content of this text, chapter 1 introduces the key terms and relationships between them, serving as the foundation for the ensuing analysis. Aquinas considers friendship to be the best kind of union between two people and thus the highest form of love. He offers a rich account of the nature of friendship in terms of different kinds of unions relevant to any act, and then habit, of love. The union of similitude is the metaphysical basis allowing for an act of love; the union of affection concerns the desire for the final union—that is, the union of possession or real union with the beloved. As a kind of love, Aquinas affirms that the will forms the basis of friendship. Cultivating and sustaining friendships, consequently, require consistent and continual appropriate acts of love. Many such appropriate acts do not involve how a lover relates to the beloved, but rather how the lover relates to himself.

Perhaps surprisingly, Aquinas does not think a person should love other human beings more than oneself. In fact, Aquinas does not think it is even possible to love another more than self. His basic reason for this claim rests not on morality, but rather on metaphysics. Union between two persons derives from unity. Two persons seek a union between them that approximates each one's substantial unity. Due to the separation of substances it presupposes, however, union can never reach the intensity afforded by unity itself. Moreover, the love of self, as the most basic activity arising from substantial unity, must be appropriately cultivated to allow both for a pleasant interior life and the possibility of true friendships with others. Among the natural impulses or inclinations of the love of self are those toward union with others. The more a person develops the appropriate love of self, the more he will be capable of and desire to love others appropriately.

Chapter 2 expands upon Aquinas's analysis of the union of similitude. A person has a greater aptitude to love another who has a greater likeness to him. Aquinas contends that any human being can love and be friends with any other human being because the shared human nature establishes a sufficient likeness between them. Nevertheless, a person is more likely to love another who possesses an initial greater likeness or similitude. Accordingly, familial relations, and particularly one's own children, tend to be the objects of greater affection. Moreover, friendships formed with kin typically have a greater natural stability and permanency relative to what Aquinas calls "friendships by choice." Friendships by choice often lead to more intense love, even if the relationships lack the stability of friendship by nature.

Interestingly, Aquinas identifies marriage as the greatest human friendship ("human" in contrast to a friendship with God). Thus, marriage forms the greatest union that two people can share. He reasons that marriage combines the strengths of a friendship by nature and a friendship by choice. Marriage has both permanency and intensity. The key notion he employs to explain why marriage allows for the best of both is indissolubility/indivisibility. By vowing absolute commitment and fidelity to one another, each spouse creates the conditions whereby the union between them comes as close as possible to each of their substantial unities. Marriage is the closest union can come to unity and thus has the potential for the most intimate and intense relationship possible.

Chapter 3 turns to the role God performs in love. Aquinas has already staked out that unity must exceed union, and therefore the love of self must exceed the love of neighbor. This would seem to commit him to the view that one should not love God more than self, for union with God cannot exceed the love based on one's own unity. However, Aquinas does contend that one ought to love God more than self. To explain how this is possible, he appeals again to metaphysics and not morality. In this case, he contends that each person's metaphysical participation in God inclines the love of self naturally to a greater love of God over self.

I argue that, for this to be consistent with the above connection between unity and union, a person's participation in God shows that substantial unity must necessarily relate to God in a fundamental way. This does not entail pantheism, but it does mean that human identity is inherently relational. Even in the context of human friendships, we begin to see that Aquinas maintains there is a built-in relationality to personal identity insofar as the love of self naturally extends to the love of others. However, in the case of God, Aquinas passes from implying to affirming. What it is be a human person is to be a being metaphysically rooted in God via participation. Moreover, the most basic activity of the love of self must relate to God if it is to be proper. Relating to God in love takes on two proper forms for Aquinas: natural love of God through the virtue of religion and the supernatural love of God through the virtue of charity.

Chapters 4 and 5 first examine the deformation and then the proper promotion of the love of God. In terms of both the deformation and promotion, each necessarily affects first the love of self and then the love of neighbor. As the first chapter establishes, Aquinas affirms that the love of others depends upon a proper love of self. The love of self cannot be proper without the proper love for God. Thus, if a person fails to love God appropriately, it will lead to damaged self-love, which undermines the ability to relate to others in love. Conversely, if a person loves God rightly, his self-love will be proper and will naturally extend toward union with others.

Chapter 4, then, treats sin as the generic way a person fails to cultivate the love of God. For Aquinas, a prideful improper self-love constitutes the root of all sin. In effect, through improper self-love, a person attempts to forsake his relational identity for one of immanence. Selfishness, self-preoccupation, and self-concern become the norm through pride. However, since this goes against one's true metaphysical identity, the net result is sorrow and self-isolation. Finally, we look at the role Satan performs in Aquinas's account of the love of self. Satan takes on an inverse role relative to God. Just as God pulls the love of self toward him for a person's ultimate perfection, so Satan, through temptation, pulls the love of self toward disorder and self-isolation.

Chapter 5 addresses the proper development of all three kinds of love: love of God, love of self, and love of neighbor. For Aquinas, self-governance issues forth from self-love, or, more precisely, it is simply a part of self-love. Actively willing and acquiring goods for oneself forms two of the essential properties of the love of self. Self-governance, then, becomes the chief means by which a person unites to others in love. In order for self-governance to manifest love rightly and consistently, a person must conform to the divine will. Part of the reason for this concerns having a friendship with God, while the other part concerns the link between conforming to the goodness of God through love: proper self-love requires the proper love of God. As the love of God perfects the love of self, a person will more readily seek and form unions with others.

In chapter 6, I explore the notion of subjectivity and offer a revised version of my argument that Aquinas affirms something like it, particularly in terms of his account of the love of self. This revised argument is the fruit of the analyses conducted in the previous chapters, as well as the work of Therese Scarpelli Cory. I also treat Linda Zagzebski's notion of omnisubjectivity. She considers the notion of God's grasp of everything a person knows from that person's first-person perspective to be both an essential mark of God and something missing from traditional natural theological accounts of the divine nature, including Aquinas's. I argue that Aquinas affirms something similar, though not identical, to what Zagzebski proposes. Last, I focus on how charity, as friendship with God, offers the full perfection of personal subjectivity.

In terms of the development of ideas within Aquinas and associated textual considerations, both the writings from the late 1250s to the mid-1260s, as evidenced by several texts, including the *Summa contra Gentiles* (*ScG*),[3] and later writings from the late 1260s until the end of his life, as evidenced by a variety of texts including

---

3. Jean-Pierre Torrell, OP, summarizing scholarship on the matter, places the *ScG* within the timeframe of 1259–64; Torell, *Saint Thomas Aquinas*, vol. 1, *The Person and His Work*, trans. Robert Royal (Washington, D.C.: The Catholic University of America Press, 1996), 101–4.

the *Summa Theologiae* (*ST*), affirm not only the threefold distinction of the love of God, self, and others, but also the structure and relationships among the three. There are two significant developments within Aquinas's notion of love itself—namely, the relationship between love and desire and the role of form in love. In the *Commentary on the Sentences of Peter Lombard*, Aquinas contends that desire precedes love, while in his later writings, he contends that love precedes desire.[4] Second, in the same commentary, Aquinas argues that love involves a transformation in terms of the object of love imparting its form in the lover. In later writings he does not speak in terms of form, but rather in terms of love as *complacentia* or the affectivity in response to an understood good.[5] These developments do not have, as far as I can tell, a notable impact on how Aquinas characterizes the three loves of God, self, and others as well as the relationships between them.

In keeping with the previous discussion, I do not employ the texts of Aquinas chronologically. The dominant sources from which I draw are the *Summa Theologiae* and *Summa contra Gentiles*. I also use his scripture commentaries. In the case of the latter, with the exception of the *Literal Exposition on Job* discussed in chapter 4, I draw exclusively from his New Testament works, and only those for which the authenticity is confirmed.[6] While these later works do not add so much to Aquinas's account of the nature of love *qua* love, as the love of God, self, and neighbor forms a key thread of scripture—if not *the* key thread of scripture—his associated commentaries do much to articulate the relationship among the three loves. While the dating of these works is not settled, the gospel commentaries coin-

---

4. For a good analysis of this change, see Christopher J. Malloy, "Thomas on the Order of Love and Desire," *Thomist* 71, no. 1 (2007): 65–87.

5. See Michael Sherwin, OP, *By Knowledge and by Love: Charity and Knowledge in the Moral Theology of St. Thomas Aquinas* (Washington, D.C.: The Catholic University of America Press, 2005), chap. 3.

6. Of particular note, I do use the *Commentary on the First Letter of Saint Paul to the Corinthians*. However, I do not use the lost sections supplemented by the text of Peter of Tarentaise—namely, the commentary for chapters 7:10–10.

cide with the *Summa Theologiae*, while the Pauline commentaries might predate the *Summa contra Gentiles*.[7] Some of them might have been initially composed between 1259 and 1268 and then revisited in 1272–73.[8]

In terms of Latin sources and translations, I have sought to use the standard translations available. In instances where more than one exist, I have opted for the most literal version. For the passages cited, I have consulted Leonine editions when possible. As Leonine editions of the New Testament commentaries are not available, I have used the Latin text supplied by the Aquinas Institute for the Study of Sacred Doctrine and consulted the Marietti editions on which they are based. The Aquinas Institute uses the Marietti editions for each commentary I cite. The only caveat is the *Commentary on the Gospel of Matthew*; as the Marietti text is incomplete, it also uses texts discovered by the Leonine Commission and confirmed as authentic.[9] However, the only passages I use from this work are present in the 1951 Marietti edition. Last, I accessed both the Leonine and Marietti texts at www.corpusthomisticum.org.

---

7. "It is not known exactly which of the books of the Bible Aquinas commented on during [his first assignment to Paris] (probably some epistles of Paul), but he was faithful to this obligation during his life, and several of his commentaries have been conserved: aside from *Isaiah*, *Jeremiah*, and *Lamentations*, the following courses must be mentioned: (*Lectures* or *Expositions*) *On Job* (Orvieto: 1261–65), *On Matthew* (Paris: 1269–70), *On John* (Paris: 1270–72), *On the Psalms* (Naples: 1273). It is difficult to know exactly the dates for the commentaries on the epistles of Paul"; Torrell, "Life and Works," in *The Oxford Handbook of Aquinas*, ed. Brian Davies and Eleonore Stump (Oxford: Oxford University Press, 2012): 15–32; quote from 17. In *Saint Thomas Aquinas*, he states, "The questions about these works are numerous and they will remain so for a long time until the critical edition of these texts will have allowed us to replace hypotheses, if not always with certitude, then at least with more certain data" (197).

8. Torrell, *Saint Thomas Aquinas*, 250–57.

9. In the notes on the text, it is stated that "the Latin text used in this volume is based on the 1951 Marietti edition, with the missing texts of Matthew 5:11–6:8 and 6:14–19 taken from texts that were found by the Leonine Commission and confirmed to be authentic." Thomas Aquinas, *Commentary on the Gospel of Matthew*, trans. Jeremy Holmes and Beth Mortensen, ed. Aquinas Institute (Lander, Wyo.: Aquinas Institute for the Study of Sacred Doctrine, 2013).

The Metaphysical Foundations of Love

1

Love as a Unitive Force

UNION AND FRIENDSHIP

In its most generic sense, love forms the basic movement toward a given end. In this sense of the term, Aquinas maintains that love is not unique to persons. Anything that strives and seeks does so on account of love. In human nature, this generic moving force accounts for natural inclinations and instinctual strivings and is the basis for sense appetites. However, love in the fully personal sense as applicable to angels, human beings, and, analogically, God, involves seeking and choosing goods as apprehended by the intellect. More specifically, personal love is the proper act of the rational appetite or will. The will's innate tendency or motion inclines toward goods as apprehended by the intellect, and an act of the will is the choice for such a good.

When a person through his will chooses a good, what he seeks, in Aquinas's terminology, is union with the good. Aquinas invokes the principle of Dionysius that love is a uniting and binding force. All love seeks a real union with the good sought. For much of everyday willing, this just means a person wants to have some given object for personal use or enjoyment—for instance, a sandwich to eat or a book to read. However, at a more important level, persons desire union with, to be united to, other persons. This might simply be an occasion for use or enjoyment, but the existence of other persons allows for something more meaningful: interpersonal union. To clarify the difference in terms of what and how one desires, Aquinas distinguishes between two kinds, or more precisely, two dimensions of love: love of concupiscence and the love of friendship. When Aquinas uses these descriptions, he does not mean that the love a person might have *for* concupiscence or *for* friendship. Rather, he intends two different directions within an act of love.

> As the Philosopher says (*Rhet.* Ii. 4), *to love is to wish good to someone*. Hence the movement of love has a twofold tendency: towards the good which a man wishes to someone,—to himself or to another, and towards that to which he wishes some good. Accordingly, man has love of concupiscence towards the good that he wishes to another, and love of friendship, towards him to whom he wishes good.[1]

On a first pass, we might think Aquinas is simply saying something like the following: the love of concupiscence is willing a good for one's own sake, while the love of friendship is willing the good for another's sake. However, this does not quite capture Aquinas's distinction, for any act of love always involves both dimensions. In the case of willing a good to oneself, a person wills the good for his own sake. In other words, he wills what he wills because it is useful or enjoyable *for him*. He wills the good to himself with a love of friendship, but the person to whom he is willing the good is himself. As we will expand upon later, the love of friendship toward oneself forms what Aquinas means by the love of self. To love another person with a love of concupiscence involves willing for oneself the other person as useful or pleasant to the lover in some way. Consequently, to love others *only* with a love of concupiscence more or less equates to selfish love. On the other hand, loving another person with a love of friendship—willing the good to him for his own sake—constitutes the basis of unselfish love.

In terms of union, in the love of concupiscence the lover seeks

---

1. Thomas Aquinas, *Summa Theologica*, trans. Fathers of the English Dominican Province (Allen, Tex.: Christian Classics, 1948), I-II, q. 26, a. 4.

a real union with the good willed. Accordingly, the love still forms a unitive force, but the union is not with another person. Only in the case of a love of friendship directed toward another person can the kind of real union sought culminate in true interpersonal union. Such real union proves to be the chief effect of love, in Aquinas's view. However, real union is preceded by two other forms of union and thus gives us a total of three: union of similitude, union of affection, and union of possession.[2]

In the case of a person loving anything, the intellect judges an object to be fitting in some way, the will desires it, and if gained, the person gains satisfaction through the real possession of the thing. Aquinas characterizes the three unions as follows:

> There is a union which causes love; and this is substantial union, as regards the love with which one loves oneself; while as regards the love wherewith one loves other things, it is the union of likeness.... There is also a union which is essentially love itself. This union is according to the bond of affection, and is likened to substantial union, inasmuch as the lover stands to the object of his love, as to something belonging to himself.... Again there is a union, which is the effect of love. This is real union, which the lover seeks with the object of his love.[3]

In terms of the love of persons, we find the same three unions, but with a greater emphasis on the union of likeness/similitude. Let us unpack these unions exclusively in terms of interpersonal love.

In the earlier passage, Aquinas makes a distinction within the union of similitude. Prior to any act of love, an underlying metaphysical union must allow for its possibility. In the case of an individual's love for himself, it is substantial union, which Aquinas also refers to as "unity." In the case of two things, there must be some shared like-

---

2. Christopher Malloy states, "Love is the second of these unions—union of affection. Love depends on the first union, and it impels (through desire) towards the last union, in which it rests (by delight). The union of similitude is the fittingness or compatibility of one thing for another, without which love is not possible.... So, both union of similitude and cognitive recognition of that similitude are necessary conditions for love. Hence, the union of similitude precedes love"; "Thomas on the Order of Love and Desire," 68.

3. *ST* I-II, q. 28, a. 1.

ness, the union of similitude that serves as the foundation for the subsequent union of affection. This latter union constitutes love's attractive, appetitive, and affective dimensions. Within this affective bond the lover relates to the beloved as another self and wills the good to the beloved not for the lover's sake, but for the sake of the beloved. Last, the affective bond tends toward real union with the beloved—the union of possession. The lover experiences joy as the natural effect of being with the beloved.

As the metaphysical basis for love, the nature of union grounds the possibility of love, determines the kinds of love possible, and shapes love's ultimate fulfillment. The metaphysics of union, as we will see, permeates a good deal of Aquinas's understanding not only of friendship, but also of healthy self-love and the necessary role God plays in the nature of love itself. In terms of the love of God, both its natural and supernatural principles depend upon considerations of union. Let us look at friendship before we turn to the love of self and love of God, as Aquinas's thoughts on friendship are likely the most accessible and least controversial.

Aquinas follows Aristotle in distinguishing three kinds of friendship based on what is loved in the other and how it is loved.[4] Friendships of utility or use derive from the (ideally) mutual benefit the persons find in one another. The good loved in the friendship is not the person as perfected by virtue, but something that is useful to both. For instance, two neighbors might share tools with one another, and such sharing constitutes nearly the entirety of the relationship. Friendships of pleasure proceed from an enjoyment of similar activities. Again, the good loved in friendship is not the person but the pleasure. In this case, two neighbors enjoy watching football together. True or complete friendship involves the love of the other's virtue—that is, the love of the other as person. The first two forms of friendship, while involving the mutual association of persons, involve only the love of concupiscence. Such friends do not primarily

---

4. See *ST* I-II, q. 27, a. 3.

love the other for the sake of the other, but rather love the other for their own sake.

True friendship requires the love of friendship because to love the beloved's virtue is to love the beloved as person. Virtue is that which perfects the person, or, to put it more strongly, virtue amounts to the person as fully actualized or at least tending toward full actualization. Each specific virtue perfects a given aspect of the person, and complete virtue integrates and perfects the person as an individual being. The love of friendship thereby has the capacity to produce real personal union beyond mere superficial association. My analysis of Aquinas uses true friendship as the point of departure and basis of the nature of friendship. Here I follow Aquinas's methodology of treating the complete or perfect instance of a thing to best understand its nature. Commenting on Aristotle, Aquinas speaks to this method in light of virtue and friendship.

For what is the perfect being in any order of reality must be considered a measure in that order, because all other things are judged more or less perfect according as they approach or recede from what is most perfect. Consequently, since virtue is the proper perfection of man and the virtuous man is perfect in the human species, this should be taken as the measure in all man's affairs.[5]

The love of true, virtuous friendship culminates in the real union of persons as persons.

Friendship begins with the union of similitude—a similitude that each human being shares with every other human being. Thus, from the metaphysical perspective, any human being serves as a potential partner in friendship. However, Aquinas adds that the more one has in common with another increases the likelihood of the development of an authentic friendship. In turn, when the intellect judges another person as a suitable good, the will can respond with an act of love. If the lover only seeks to use or enjoy the other person

---

5. Aquinas, *Commentary on Aristotle's Nicomachean Ethics*, trans. C. I. Litzinger, OP (Notre Dame: Ind.: Dumb Ox, 1993), 1803. This work is dated to 1271–72; see also Torrell, *Saint Thomas Aquinas*, 227–29.

as a means for one's own enjoyment, then a full friendship will not develop. Friendship requires the unselfish love of friendship.

Although the love of friendship forms the essential key note of friendship proper, taken by itself, it does not constitute a sufficient condition for friendship. A person can will the good to another for the latter's own sake out of goodwill or benevolence and even seek the good for the other out of beneficence. However, if the recipient is unaware or uninterested in the agent, the relationship is not one of friendship. Aquinas contends that true friendship requires two further necessary conditions—namely, those of habit and reciprocity. Before turning to these conditions, let us expand upon the importance of the love of friendship.

While not sufficient, the love of friendship nevertheless forms the central and necessary condition to friendship. The centrality of this love rests upon that which is loved in the beloved. In the love of friendship, a person seeks the personhood of the other as the proper object of that love.

> Now friendship cannot be extended to virtues or any accidents ... because friendship makes a man want his friend to exist and to have what is good. But accidents do not exist on their own, nor have they goodness on their own; being and well-being are theirs only when they exist in substances. Hence, we do want virtues and accidents to exist, yet not for themselves, but for a *subject* to which we want being or well-being to come by way of those accidents.[6]

A lover does not relate principally to the qualities of the beloved in friendship. Neither does the lover relate in such a way to the beloved's intellect, will, or any other power. Rather, the lover loves the subject of those powers and qualities. Aquinas highlights this point another way by affirming that personhood makes one "incommunicable and distinct from others."[7] Each person, while possessing

---

6. Aquinas, *Scriptum super libros Sententiarum Petri Lombardi*, from *On Love and Charity: Readings from the "Commentary on the Sentences of Peter Lombard,"* selected and trans. Peter Kwasniewki, Thomas Bolin, OSB, and Joseph Bolin (Washington, D.C: The Catholic University of America Press, 2008), III, d. 28, a. 1. Italics are in the original, which will be the case for all subsequently cited passages containing italics.

7. Aquinas, *On the Power of God*, trans. English Dominican Fathers (Westminster,

communicable human nature and repeatable qualities, exists first and foremost as a unique person. Everything else is particularized as modifying *this* individual person. In the love of friendship, a person does not merely love the replaceable qualities of the beloved but rather the unique subject who anchors and is expressed through these qualities.[8]

For this personhood-directed love to become integrated into friendship, two further basic conditions need to be satisfied. First, in friendship, the love must become habitual. While a person might have occasional moments of willing the good to someone, such as a stranger or neighbor, only if he wills the good consistently might he have a friendship with the other. Second, the beloved must reciprocate the same kind of love, forming a mutual love between them. If all of these conditions are met, two persons are friends in the full Thomistic sense of the term.

The union of possession or real union of friends pertains most essentially to the personal presence or the mutual indwelling of shared love. Aquinas follows the scriptural tradition by identifying the heart as the unique, interior core of personal existence. Thus, the heart is the proper and most intimate nexus point of a deep friendship. Two intimate friends, as Aquinas maintains in the *Summa contra Gentiles*, make "one heart of two" by entering into and sharing their hearts with one another,[9] dwelling within one another in a reciprocal manner. In the *Summa Theologiae*, Aquinas offers a detailed account of just how intimate the experience of mutual indwelling can be.

Md.: Newman Press, 1952), q. 9, a. 4. This work, along with the first beginning of the *Summa Theologiae*, was composed in the second half of the 1260s; see also Torrell, *Saint Thomas Aquinas*, 161–64.

8. Linda Trinkaus Zagzebski offers a helpful analysis that focuses on the repeatability of qualities versus the nonrepeatability of persons in "The Uniqueness of Persons," *Journal of Religious Ethics* 29, no. 3 (2001): 401–23; see also John Crosby, *The Selfhood of the Human Person* (Washington, D.C.: The Catholic University of America Press, 1996), chap. 2.

9. Aquinas, *Summa contra Gentiles*, trans. Charles J. O'Neil (Notre Dame, Ind.: University of Notre Dame Press, 1975), IV, c. 21, p. 5.

This effect of mutual indwelling may be understood as referring both to the apprehensive and to the appetitive power. Because, as to the apprehensive power, the beloved is said to be in the lover, inasmuch as the beloved abides in the apprehension of the lover ... while the lover is said to be in the beloved, according to apprehension, inasmuch as the lover is not satisfied with a superficial apprehension of the beloved, but strives to gain an intimate knowledge of everything pertaining to the beloved, so as to penetrate into his very soul.... As the appetitive power, the object loved is said to be in the lover, inasmuch as it is in his affections, by a kind of complacency: causing him either to take pleasure in it, or in its good, when present; or, in the absence of the object loved, by his longing, to tend towards it with the love of concupiscence, or towards the good that he wills to the beloved, with the love of friendship: not indeed from any extrinsic cause (as when we desire one thing on account of another, or wish good to another on account of something else), but because the complacency in the beloved is rooted in the lover's heart. For this reason we speak of love as being *intimate*; and of *the bowels of charity*.[10]

In short, the fully realized real union of persons differs from the real union with nonpersonal beings insofar as the latter do not have an interior life. There is nothing to be "in." A person has a real union with a plant or cat when he owns it, and this union becomes fully realized when physically present with the thing. It is of course possible that human relationships never rise above an analogous copresence with another person. However, such physical copresence does not satisfy the conditions for personal union.

Eleonore Stump discusses this dimension to Aquinas's account of interpersonal love in terms of a minimal personal presence of the conscious awareness of another conscious being. In friendship, personal presence must be marked by joint attention. In addition to joint attention, a certain closeness is required between friends. She states:

Propinquity alone is not sufficient for closeness, not even propinquity prolonged or often repeated.... Just adding conversation to propinquity will not produce closeness; general benevolence plus conversation and

---

10. *ST* I-II, q. 28, a. 2.

propinquity is not enough either.... Paula's being close to Jerome thus not only involves certain states of mind and will in both Paula and Jerome, but also involves relational attitudes on Jerome's part. It involves Jerome's having desires about Paula's desires about Jerome and her understanding of him, and it requires his having a need and desire for her.[11]

Propinquity does not suffice for friendship. Personal presence minimally involves a mutual awareness of two people as people. As the tendency of love toward union progresses, it must go deeper into what makes the person a personal being in general and specifically in terms of his beliefs and desires. For Aquinas, real possession does not occur until the lover encounters and enters into the heart of the other; the degree of intimacy is measured in large part by the extent to which the heart of the lovers is mutually known and enjoyed.

Addressing further the nature and intensity of the affective and real union, Aquinas treats additional effects of love: ecstasy, melting, delight (and by extension, sadness), and fervor. He defines ecstasy as being "placed outside oneself."[12] The natural dynamism of the love of friendship is toward the beloved. A person's thoughts and actions become directed to the good of the other. In effect, ecstasy, particularly mutual ecstasy, is the mechanism making mutual indwelling possible. Aquinas asks whether the outward direction of love "wounds" the lover.[13] He responds that inappropriate love can indeed hurt and worsen the lover, but proper love—the will's and emotions' adapting and uniting to a good person—serves to perfect the lover and beloved. To enter into such a union, the heart of either lover cannot be frozen or resistant to ecstasy. "Melting denotes a softening of the heart, whereby the heart shows itself to be ready for the entrance of the beloved."[14]

Ecstasy and the mutual indwelling to which it leads serve as a great cause of delight. Aquinas uses "delight" as a generic term mean-

---

11. Eleonore Stump, *Wandering in Darkness: Narrative and the Problem of Suffering* (Oxford: Oxford University Press, 2010), 119, 123.
12. *ST* I-II, q. 28, a. 3.
13. *ST* I-II, q. 28, a. 5.
14. Ibid.

ing any affective enjoyment of a good. If the delight involves sense appetites, then it conveys pleasure and such. If the delight involves the satisfaction of the will, then it involves joy.[15] In the case of friendship, delight comes in both forms, but predominately in the latter. Aquinas further specifies two sources of joy in friendship:

> For joy is caused by love, either through the presence of the thing loved, or because the proper good of the thing loved exists and endures in it; and the latter is the case chiefly in the love of benevolence, whereby a man rejoices in the well-being of his friend, though he be absent.[16]

While the absence of the beloved can cause sadness insofar as the lover fervently wills the continued full presence of the beloved, a certain joy of friendship persists even here. Even in the absence of the beloved, the lover continues to experience the beloved actively as the object of his willing. He wills the good of his friend and takes delight in the goodness of his friend and friendship.

Perhaps a bit more concretely and specifically, Aquinas attends to communication and conversation, "really to converse with the friend,"[17] as proper to friendship. Conversation serves as the practical means by which friends enter into each other's hearts. Aquinas adds an additional mark of friendship or, as a special mode of the present one, the revelation of secrets. The revelation of intimate things about oneself in friendship both speaks to the bond of trust between friends and acts to intensify that bond.

Frequently, Aquinas offers Aristotle's list of five essential marks of friendship to underscore the above considerations, while adding one further property—namely, that of concord.

> Every friend wishes his friend to be and to live; secondly, he desires good things for him; thirdly, he does good things to him; fourthly, he takes pleasure in his company; fifthly, he is of one mind with him, rejoicing and sorrowing in almost the same things.[18]

---

15. *ST* I-II, q. 31, a. 3.
16. *ST* II-II, q. 28, a. 1.
17. *ScG* IV, c. 22, p. 2.
18. *ST* II-II, q. 5, a. 7.

Friends experience a mutual longing, benevolence, beneficence, delight, and concord. At the most basic level, a lover longs for his beloved to continue to be and live. The final cause of this longing, though, pertains to the continued mutual indwelling of friendship permeated by the marks of ecstasy, conversing, sharing, trust, and fervor. As a further specification of longing for the continued presence of the beloved, benevolence concerns the willing of particular goods for the betterment of the beloved's existence. Benevolence's natural tendency culminates in beneficent action—seeking those goods for the beloved with a love of friendship. In terms of affective dimension of the closeness of mutual indwelling, Aquinas speaks to the delight and consolation afforded by the presence of the beloved. Last, insofar as the union between persons develops and deepens toward unity, there is the concord of wills between them. This is not to say that lovers must agree on everything, "but only upon such goods as conduce to life, and especially upon such as are important."[19]

UNITY AND THE LOVE OF SELF

Love of others in general and friendship in particular, for Aquinas, derives from a more basic source—namely, a person's love of self. A person does and should love himself more than he loves other human beings. Aquinas is not endorsing selfishness and self-preoccupation. In fact, as we will discuss in the next section as well as in chapters 4 and 5, proper self-love functions as the antidote to selfishness and self-preoccupation. We have already discussed how the love of friendship, as opposed to loving another person solely with a love of concupiscence, of its nature seeks the good of others for their own sake. Such love should form the basis of our love of neighbors, particularly once transformed by the supernatural form of love of charity. Even in the context of charity, however, Aquinas continues to affirm that the love of self through charity must exceed the love of neighbor. We will turn to the love of others in the next section.

19. *ST* II-II, q. 29, a. 3, ad 2.

The reason for the priority of self-love over love of others is not a moral one at its root. Instead, the metaphysical difference of unity versus union determines the question of priority. Given that love between persons presupposes and proceeds from union—namely, the union of similitude—the kinds of union in question determine the direction and key characteristics of love itself. In this case, the love of others arises from a union of similitude with them. The union of similitude receives its characteristics in reference to substantial unity. Unity is the principle, while similitude is the principled. Love must respect, if you will, this underlying reality. In terms of love's finality in the union of possession, it seeks a union with another that approximates to the degree possible to the unity that undergirds it.

Let us begin to unpack these relationships in light of one of the key passages from Aquinas on the matter.

> We must hold that, properly speaking, a man is not a friend to himself, but something more than a friend, since friendship implies union, for Dionysius says (*Div Nom.* iv) that *love is a unitive force*, whereas a man is one with himself which is more than being united to another. Hence, just as unity is the principle of union, so the love with which a man loves himself is the form and root of friendship. For if we have friendship with others it is because we do unto them as we do unto ourselves, hence we read in *Ethic.* ix.4.8 that "the origin of friendly relations with others lies in our relations to ourselves."[20]

Unity sets the baseline parameters for how we should understand union. Union must be between at least two things. What makes a thing a thing is unity. In terms of Aquinas's metaphysics, we find this notion expressed in terms of the idea of oneness (*unum*) as constituting a transcendental property of being itself. Aquinas defines "one" as "undivided *being*."[21] Each being is an individual. A being of its most basic nature cannot be divided without destroying the being itself. There cannot be a true metaphysical oneness or unity between two things because such a state would violate the undividedness of the

---

20. *ST* II-II, q. 25, a. 4.
21. *ST* I, q. 11, a. 1.

things in question (such a "unity" would be severed). Love tends toward the sort of union that is possible—a union of hearts or the making "one heart of two." A complete union of hearts, as discussed earlier, involves the total sharing and mutual indwelling of the persons with one another.

As proceeding from unity, the love of self is immune to many of the issues of interpersonal love stemming from the separation or division of substances that stand as the foundation of interpersonal love. Substantial unity immediately undergirds self-love, and self-love naturally proceeds from substantial unity. "As to be one is better than to be united, so there is more oneness in love which is directed to self than in love which unites one to others."[22] In the case of animals, their naturally occurring self-love does not involve the will and intellect. Animals instinctually seek the goods conducive to their flourishing. In virtue of human nature, the self-love of the individual person does naturally involve the conscious striving for and choosing of one's own good.

While we will examine the role the love of God performs in human self-love in chapter 3, here we can speak to how self-love reflects the divine nature. From the perspective of natural theology, Aquinas holds that God loves himself and necessarily so. The object most fitting to God's will is God himself; thus, God loves himself first and foremost. In terms of sacred theology, Aquinas appeals to divine self-love in the procession of the Holy Spirit from Father and Son. All creatures imitate their creator, and human beings as created in the image and likeness of God do so to a greater degree. From both a natural and supernatural perspective, it is unsurprising that Aquinas places considerable importance on the love of self.

The ways in which an individual seeks the good for himself becomes the model or template for how he loves other persons—"we do unto them as we do unto ourselves." Focusing on the role of the will in self-love, Aquinas maintains that the love of self forms the ba-

---

22. *ST* I, q. 60, a. 3, ad 2.

sis for all other acts of the will. David Gallagher's study on the matter explains this clearly:

> Thomas holds self-love to be natural. Every person naturally loves himself with a love of friendship and wants or wills for himself, with a love of concupiscence, all the good(s) that are required for his fulfillment. That is to say, each person naturally loves beatitude of himself with a love of concupiscence. From this natural self-love arise all further acts of willing. Hence, if a person is to love another person by an act of the will, the origin of that second love will have to be explained in terms of the first and more basic love.[23]

The love of self proceeds from the will as the latter's first act of self-movement. The love of self, then, structurally precedes the love founded upon union with other things.

Since self-love involves the will, like everything else involving willing, we find more than one form of self-love. Aquinas distinguishes among three kinds of self-love: natural/common, good/proper/well-ordered, and bad/wicked/disordered. He begins with common self-love, as it is found in all human beings by nature.

> Love of self is common to all, in one way, in another way it is proper to the good; in a third way, it is proper to the wicked. For it is common to all for each one to love what he thinks himself to be. Now a man is said to be a thing, in two ways: first, in respect of his substance and nature, and, this way all think themselves to be what they are, that is, composed of a soul and body. In this way too, all men, both good and wicked, love themselves, insofar as they love their own preservation.[24]

Although the love of self as grounded in unity does not admit of the separation of substances found in interpersonal love, it still can be directed to different aspects, real or imagined, of one's self. It is this possibility that allows for proper and improper forms of self-love.

Common self-love is the basic self-relation deriving immediately from substantial unity. It can be developed positively or negatively.

---

23. David A. Gallagher, "Thomas Aquinas on Self-Love as the Basis for Love of Others," *Acta Philosophica* 8, no. 1 (1999): 29.

24. *ST* II-II, q. 25, a. 7.

Through proper self-love, a person seeks those things that contribute to the real development of human personhood. As we will consider later, proper self-love naturally extends outward. The love of self does not culminate in immanence, but rather extends outward to others. More concretely, self-love does not stop at willing goods perfective of one's own nature, but extends to the willing and seeking of goods for others, ultimately with a love of friendship.

Contrasting good and wicked self-love, Aquinas states:

> A man is said to be something in respect of some predominance, as the sovereign of a state is spoken of as being the state, and so, what the sovereign does, the state is said to do. In this way, all do not think themselves to be what they are. For the reasoning mind is the predominant part of man, while the sensitive and corporeal nature takes the second place, the former of which the Apostle calls the *inward man*, and the latter, the *outward man* (2 Cor 4:16). Now the good look upon their rational nature or the inward man as being the chief thing in them, wherefore in this way they think themselves to be what they are. On the other hand, the wicked reckon their sensitive and corporeal nature, or the outer man, to hold the first place. Wherefore, since they know not themselves aright, they do not love themselves aright, but love that they think themselves to be. But the good know themselves truly, and therefore truly love themselves.[25]

Through wicked love of self, a person seeks the bodily pleasures and material goods at the expense of the goods perfective of his properly personal nature. Wicked or disordered love of self perverts natural self-love away from the full spectrum of goods perfective of human nature, including interpersonal unions, and toward a more restricted set of goods willed solely for oneself.

Through this disordered manner of willing, wicked self-love constitutes the root of all sin. "The love of self which is the principle of sin is that which is proper to the wicked, and reaches *to the contempt of God* ... because the wicked so desire external goods as to despise spiritual goods."[26] That wicked self-love is the cause of all sin is a simple inference for Aquinas. All actions, both good and sinful, pro-

25. Ibid.
26. Ibid., ad 1.

ceed from the will. The basic act of the will is love, and all actions are motivated by love. Thus, sinful acts, while necessarily motivated by love, must be caused by disordered love. In chapter 4, we will look extensively at the role pride plays in sin. It suffices for our present purpose to note that pride and wicked self-love form two sides of the same coin. Any act of pride requires an act of disordered self-love. Pride involves an exaggerated sense of self-importance and love of that imagined self that culminate in the rejection of any authority beyond one's own will.

Well-ordered self-love properly develops and actualizes common self-love. Just as in other areas of Aquinas's ethics, through the will and virtue, a person perfects or perverts a given natural capacity or inclination. In this case, natural self-love is what nature gives to a person, so to speak, and he is free to pervert or perfect it. Aquinas contends that the process of perfecting the love of self and its term involve the same properties as found in a friendship between persons.

Due to the way Aquinas relates proper self-love to friendship, I referred to full development of proper self-love as "self-friendship" in my previous book. Some have objected to me in conversation that, since friendship must require more than one person, "self-friendship" tends toward incoherency, even if Aquinas himself uses the term analogically. Partly due to this concern some have expressed, I have replaced the term with "proper self-love." An additional reason, though, is that "self-friendship" fails to convey sufficiently the nonnegotiable priority self-love possesses over the love of others. A person's relations to himself in self-love are greater than anything found in friendship, as when Aquinas says "a man is not a friend to himself, but something more than a friend." Thus, I will use the term "proper self-love" instead of "self-friendship."[27]

27. Both Aristotle and Aquinas would dismiss objections to self-friendship simply as a terminological versus real problem. In Aquinas's commentary on Aristotle on this point, he states the following: "Then, at 'But whether a person,' he raises a question—does a man have friendship toward himself? He observes that this question must be postponed since it is a semantic problem rather than a real one. Friendship seems to ex-

In his early writings—namely, the *Commentary on the Sentences of Peter Lombard*—Aquinas draws upon the structure and properties of friendship to explain what proper self-love *entails*. He states:

> For since love in a certain way unites lover to beloved, the lover therefore stands to the beloved as if to himself or to that which concerns his perfection. But to himself and to that which belongs to him, he stands in the following ways. First, he wishes whatever concerns his perfection to be present to him; and therefore love includes *longing* for the beloved, by which the beloved's presence is desired. Second, in his affections a man turns other things back to himself and seeks for himself whatever goods are expedient for him; and so far as this is done for the beloved, love includes the *benevolence* by which someone desires good things for the beloved. Third, the things a man desires for himself he actually acquires for himself by acting; and insofar as this activity is exercised toward another, love includes *beneficence*. Fourth, to the accomplishment of whatever seems good in his sight, he gives his full consent; and insofar as this attitude comes to be toward a friend, love includes *concord* by which someone consents to things as they seem [good] to his friend.[28]

Friendship derives its nature from proper self-love. Thus, it should not be surprising that the characteristics of friendship derive their nature from ways in which a person relates to himself.

In terms of the property of longing, in a friendship between persons there is a metaphysical separation of substances. Seeking to overcome this separation, a friend longs to be with, to be united to,

---

ist among any persons who possess two or three of the characteristics mentioned. And when the friendship for others excels, it is similar to the love a man has for himself. Consequently, someone wishing to prove his friendship for another is accustomed to say 'I love you as myself.' Hence it doesn't make any difference whether the word friendship is applied to self, because the reality of friendship abundantly belongs to a man in regard to himself"; Aquinas, *Commentary on Aristotle's Nicomachean Ethics*, 1812, emphasis in original.

28. *On Love and Charity: Readings from the "Commentary on the Sentences of Peter Lombard,"* III, d. 27, q. 2, a.1. In *ST* II-II, q. 25, a. 7, Aquinas offers a similar analysis: "In this way the good love themselves, as to the inward man, because they wish the preservation thereof in its integrity, they desire good things for him, namely spiritual goods, indeed they do their best to obtain them, and they take pleasure in entering into their own hearts, because they find there good thoughts in the present, the memory of past good, and the hope of future good, all of which are sources of pleasure. Likewise they experience no clashing of wills, since their whole soul tends to one thing."

the beloved. In self-love, there is no metaphysical separation, but the love can be directed to different aspects of oneself. When self-love is proper, a person relates most fundamentally to himself as an incommunicable person. The roots of benevolence and beneficence in self-love concern willing and seeking true goods that enhance both one's nature and the integrity of one's interior life. Thus, the activity of self-governance itself derives from self-love. In friendship, delight and concord relate to the affective dimension of the experience of the other. In terms of self-love, they relate to the affective dimension of the experience of oneself. A notable absence of inner strife or discord, and in its place, the presence of a consoling interior peace, mark the inner heart of a person with well-ordered love of self.

FROM UNITY TO UNION

The key principle Aquinas expresses above is this: "Just as unity is the principle of union, so the love with which a man loves himself is the form and root of friendship." In another place, he articulates a chief consequence of this principle, stating a "man's love for himself is the model of his love for another."[29] We began this chapter with friendship instead of the love of self, as it is an easier notion to understand. However, several of the passages we have examined show Aquinas repeatedly emphasizing that friendship is, in fact, the derivative reality. The properties of the love of self are not similar to the properties of friendship; it is the other way around. The cause of the relationship between the love of self and the love of others is the underlying metaphysical relationship between unity and union.

Aquinas insists that the proper development of self-love holds the key to relating properly to others. Consequently, a good part of everyday human life and social interaction depends upon how a person cultivates self-love. This has to do with a couple of principal factors. First, the love of self provides the antidote to selfishness. In addition, the activity of self-love provides a training ground of sorts for

---

29. *ST* II-II, q. 26, a. 4, *sed contra*.

learning how to will appropriate goods to others and learning to will those goods to others for their own sake.

It might seem counterintuitive that the love of self counters selfishness, but Aquinas's reasoning on the matter is both simple and compelling.[30] In self-love, a person wills goods to himself because he apprehends that they are noble, pleasant, or useful. Once he apprehends the existence of other persons, with whom he shares a union of similitude, or more simply, individuals who have the same basic nature as himself, he is rationally committed to the idea that these goods should be willed to them also. In short, he cannot consistently will them to himself while refusing to will them to others. To do so would involve him willing them to himself precisely because he grasps their suitability for himself. Once he sees others have the same nature, he will see an analogous suitability of those same goods for others. Put positively, the love of self contains a natural inclination to extend a person's willing of goods to others, and as we will see, to will them for the sake of the other.

Aquinas expands upon this notion, commenting on the various instances in scripture that cite the precept "you shall love your neighbor as yourself." These contexts involve charity, but he typically casts his commentary in terms of the principles of natural love to explain the relationships between love of self and love of others. He uses almost every one of these occasions to reiterate that not only is the love of self naturally prior to love of neighbor, but also that we have an ethical obligation to develop both loves in that order. In other words, Aquinas is not saying that, while nature inclines human beings one way, virtue and grace counter the natural inclination with

---

30. I think my interpretation on this matter in Aquinas is right. However, my argumentative interpretation follows the structure of an argument Linda Zagzebski gives in a different context that might be influencing my take on Aquinas. She makes the case that, in the context of forming beliefs, a conscientious epistemic agent is rationally committed to a default trust in the beliefs of other conscientious thinkers insofar as both have the same cognitive nature; see Zagzebski, "Ethical and Epistemic Egoism and the Ideal of Autonomy," *Episteme: A Journal of Social Epistemology* 4, no. 3 (2007): 252. She expands upon the argument in *Epistemic Authority: A Theory of Trust, Authority, and Autonomy in Belief* (Oxford: Oxford University Press, 2012).

an opposed tendency to promote love of others over love of self. As virtue and grace build upon and perfect nature, so charity builds upon and perfects the priority of the love of self over others. Obviously, wicked self-love remains the obstacle in all of this, as it is the root of sin, but proper self-love is the necessary condition for virtue.

In his *Commentary on Galatians*, Aquinas maintains the following:

> He [Christ] says, *as yourself*, not *as much as yourself*, because according to the order of charity a man should love himself more than his neighbor. Now this is explained in three ways: first, as referring to the genuineness of the love. For to love is to will good to someone: hence we are said to love both the one to whom we will a good and the very good which we will to someone; but not in the same way. For when I will a good to myself, I love myself absolutely for myself, but the good which I will to myself, I do not love for itself but for myself. Accordingly, I love my neighbor as myself in the same way that I love myself, when I will him a good for his sake, and not because it is useful or pleasant for me. In a second way, as referring to the justice of love. For each thing is inclined to want for itself that which is most eminent in it; but in man, understanding and reason are the most eminent. He, therefore, loves himself who wants for himself the good of understanding and reason. Accordingly, you then love your neighbor as yourself, when you will him the good of understanding and reason. In a third way, as referring to order, i.e., that just as you love yourself for the sake of God, so you love your neighbor for the sake of God, that he may attain God.[31]

We will discuss in subsequent chapters the role the love of God plays in the love one has for oneself and others. For now, let us focus on the first two points. In short, the various ways that a person relates to himself forms the template for how he relates to others.

Proper self-love both sets the standard for how to love others and imparts the ability and inclination to do so. What it means to love one's neighbor truly is to will the good to him for his own sake. To love anything striking us as useful or pleasant with a love of con-

---

31. Aquinas, *Commentary on the Letters of Saint Paul to the Galatians*, trans. Fr. Fabian R. Larcher, OP, and M. L. Lamb, ed. J. Mortensen and E. Alarcon (Lander, Wyo.: Aquinas Institute for the Study of Sacred Doctrine, 2012), 305; compare Aquinas, *Commentary on the Gospel of Matthew*, 1816–19.

cupiscence is easy enough to do. With the love of concupiscence, a person desires the thing in question because it enables him to extend his own interests or gives him pleasure. Loving other persons under such conditions with a love of concupiscence is also an easy thing to do. A person loving his neighbor out of a love of concupiscence loves his neighbor insofar as the neighbor fixes his car, or because he enjoys the neighbor's well-stocked refrigerator. In both of these cases, the interpersonal relationships represent more an extension of a person's own interests than a true loving union.

To love another person in the most appropriate way and in the manner effecting the greatest union is to love him with a love of friendship. The lover loves the beloved not primarily because it is useful (although it could be), or because it is pleasant (although it could be), but because the lover wills goods to the beloved for the beloved's own sake. Moreover, the lover knows how to do this precisely because he already wills goods to himself in such a way. Thus, the proper love of neighbor—the love of friendship for one's neighbor—represents not an extension of one's own interests but an extension of the way a person loves oneself.[32] Given the fact that the love of friendship extends the way one loves oneself to others, it would seem that everyone should be able to do it with ease. Aquinas thinks a version of this point is the case insofar as all persons have the resources for knowing how to love others with a love of friendship. However, loving another person for the other's own sake is only possible if the love of self is proper.

32. There is a strand of scholarship that maintains that Aquinas's analysis cannot escape an inherent selfishness in rooting the love of others in the love of self. In effect, the claim is that any love of another would have to be in the form of the love of concupiscence. David M. Gallagher rebuts this line of interpretation in "Thomas Aquinas on Self-Love as the Basis for Love of Others." He points out that through the "unity" we have with others, we will goods to them for their own sake but still from self-love. I call attention to this both to express gratitude for Gallagher's work but also to note that he uses the term "unity" in a looser sense than I do. Gallagher contends we can have a unity with another, for which I use the term "union." I think the clearest interpretation of Aquinas is to preserve "unity" for the metaphysical description of literal oneness and "union" for cases of two or more individuals. As we will discuss in the next chapter, though, union admits of degrees. Consequently, some unions are closer to unity than others.

We begin to see Aquinas's insistence on the necessity of proper love of self with his second remark concerning the justice of love. The wicked person's self-love predominately loves the inferior characteristics of himself at the expense of his full personal self as a rational being. He loves the wrong sorts of things, or at least, he loves things that, while good, are loved at the expense of higher goods. In addition, as seen in the previous passage on wicked self-love causing sin, he increasingly grows prideful in his love. Thus, even under the best of circumstances, when a person attempts to will goods to another with the love of friendship, the goods in question will not be appropriate. He will gravitate toward the willing of goods perfective of the bodily and material aspects of the other at the expense of those goods perfective of the other's fully personal nature. Moreover, the tendency of pride prompts him to view other persons more and more as means for his use or pleasure instead of beings to be loved for their own sake.

We will expand upon these themes as we go, but consider here the following description of the negative consequences of wrong action from *De Veritate*: "Every being has the act of existing in the proportion in which it approaches God by likeness. But according as it is found to be unlike Him, it approaches non-existence."[33] Given the transcendental nature of unity or *unum*, the less being one has, the less unity one has. Wicked self-love undermines a person at the most basic level by weakening a person's unity. Such disintegration works against forming unions with others. Stump notes the following connection between integration and love of others:

To the extent to which a person is divided against himself, to that extent he cannot be at one with others either. The lack of internal integration is therefore inimical to the union desired in love.... If he wills whole-

---

33. Aquinas, *On Truth*, trans. Robert W. Schmidt, SJ (Indianapolis, Ind.: Hackett, 1994), q. 23, a. 7. The passage continues: "And the same must be said of all the attributes which are found both in God and in creatures. Hence His intellect is the measure of all knowledge; His goodness, of all goodness; and, to speak more to the point, His good will, of every good will. Every good will is therefore good by reason of its being conformed to the divine good will."

heartedly, he will *ipso facto* be integrated in the will. A person who lacks internal integration in the will is, then, a person who does not will what he needs to will in order to be internally integrated. Consequently, the fact that others are kept from being close to him because of the lack of internal integration in his will is a result of the state of his own will.[34]

The lack of interior integration, having disordered self-love, prevents a person from loving others with a true love of friendship.

Through the properties of benevolence and beneficence, a person marked by proper self-love wills those goods to oneself contributing to one's full personal development. These goods enhance one's substantial unity. The more a person seeks and acquires true goods, the more being he has. Unity or *unum* as a transcendental property follows the same rule. A person has greater substantial unity the more goods he acquires. This has to do in large part with the way the will must conform to the good. We will expand upon this notion in chapter 4. For now, due to a person's experience and familiarity with willing and acquiring truly perfective goods, he is in a position to will those same kinds of goods to others and to do so with a love of friendship. Proper self-love forms the basic pattern, both in terms of the kinds of good willed and the manner by which they are willed, for the love of others. As discussed in the first section, merely loving another person appropriately does not constitute a full friendship, but it is the foundation of an appropriate loving union with them. In many cases, it will then lead to a mutual friendship.

To summarize this chapter, love is a uniting and binding force. It depends upon the metaphysical connection between unity and union. Unity with oneself forms the basis for the love of self. Human beings are naturally drawn toward forming unions with one another. The quality of such unions is measured by its approximation to a person's experience of his own unity or substantial oneness grounded in the love of self. As unity is prior to union, the self-love proceeding from unity naturally proceeds and sets the pattern for the love tending toward union with others.

---

34. Stump, *Wandering in Darkness*, 130.

We still must address the biggest part of the love equation—namely, the love a person has for God. The love of God likewise finds its foundation in considerations of unity and union. Before we turn to the love of God, let us look more closely at the role unity and union perform in human relationships. Insofar as union, particularly the union of similitude, admits of degrees, so too do the consequent interpersonal unions and love relationships founded upon the similitude.

2

Degrees of Union

DISTINCTIONS PERTAINING TO THE UNIONS OF SIMILITUDE AND POSSESSION

The union of similitude forms the metaphysical foundation for a genuine love of friendship. A person loves another person only on the condition that he perceives some likeness and equality to himself in the other. Ultimately, as human nature satisfies the baseline condition of similitude, the connection between similitude and love entails the possibility of loving any rational being with the aim of forming a real interpersonal union with him; every human being *qua* human shares a fundamental equality with one another. In addition to the baseline condition, Aquinas affirms that the degree of similitude, both present and perceived, influences the likelihood of forming a real union with another. Moreover, this same degree affects the quality of the love. The greater the similitude between persons, the more likely love is between them. Also, a greater similitude encourages a greater stability and permanency to the love. Aquinas makes a variety of distinctions on both the natural and supernatural levels in regard to these connections. This chapter will examine some of the key aspects of this account and culminate in a treatment of marriage, which Aquinas considers to be the framework allowing for the most stable and intense love relationship between human persons.

Aquinas treats the order of charity in both his *Disputed Question on Charity* and the *Summa Theologiae*. In both, he first lays out the threefold order of love we have been considering: God, self, and others. He then considers the question of whether it is appropriate to love some people more than others. While the context is charity, like we saw in the previous chapter with the passages from his commentaries on scripture, most of his reasoning draws from natural principles, though with one notable difference, which we will discuss momentarily.

In *ST* II-II, q. 26, a. 7, Aquinas considers the issue of whether one should love morally good people more than those with whom one is united (*coniunctiores*). In his response, he distinguishes between two perspectives of love and charity: object and agent. The object of love accounts for the kind of love it is. God, and by extension all human beings as related to him, is the proper object of charity. Thereby, a person should will, out of love, the good of beatitude to those most connected to God—namely, those who are morally upright. In contrast to this, the other perspective does not pertain to the object, but to the power of the agent to love. The power accounts for the intensity of the love—the rapidity and force by which the power seeks its end. In the case of love, the end sought is real union with the beloved. In terms of intensity, Aquinas argues that we should have a greater love for those united to us over the morally good or any other category.

Here again, Aquinas is speaking of two kinds of union, one as principle and the other as term. The *coniunctiores* are those with whom one has a greater union of similitude. When one loves them with greater intensity, one seeks the greatest possible real union or union of possession with them. Real union conveys both the continued union and an ever-greater union with the beloved. The greater union of similitude forms the principle of the agent's love. The union of possession, desired generally in proportion to the greater similitude, forms the term of the love.

In the next article, Aquinas employs a distinction between

Degrees of Union

friendship of natural origin and friendship by choice. Obviously, any love of friendship as rooted in the will involves choice, but here the distinction pertains to the reality of varying similitudes.

> It is evident that the union arising from natural origin is prior to, and more stable than, all others, because it is something affecting the very substance, whereas other unions supervene and may cease altogether. Therefore the friendship of kindred is more stable, while other friendships may be stronger in respect of that which is proper to each of them.[1]

It is possible for a person to form friendships with anyone by choice, as the similitude satisfies the most fundamental condition for such union. Moreover, friendships from choice have the potential to become stronger than those of natural origin, particularly if there are shared circumstances and goals between the friends. Aquinas uses the example of the bonds of soldiers fighting alongside one another in battle as an example of such intensity; we might think of fellow colleagues who have a prima facie comfort with one another due to their common form of life. These sorts of circumstances do not pertain to the natural union of similitude, but as conventional layers on top of it, so to speak. These circumstances often encourage friendships of choice, which represent friendships often allowing for a great intensity of love.

Although friendships based on choice can achieve great intensity, Aquinas nonetheless considers friendships based on natural origin to be more stable and permanent relative to friendships by choice. The reason for this pertains directly to considerations of natural similitude. One has, by nature, a greater likeness with those to whom one is related and thus has a stronger initial reason for friendship. In turn, this serves as a more solid basis for the perseverance of the friendship relative to friendships of choice.

Aquinas employs the general principle stating that "the union arising from natural origin is prior to, and more stable than, all others, because it is something affecting the very substance" to illus-

---

1. *ST* II-II, q. 26, a. 8.

trate how nature encourages, if you will, human beings to have closer bonds of love with some people over others. In his *Commentary on Galatians*, he puts it as follows:

> Since the intensity of an act results from the principle of action, and the principle of action is union and similarity, we ought to love in a higher degree and more intensely those who are more like us and more closely united to us.[2]

This does not mean that nature inclines us to shun other groups. Basic human nature, which all share, also grounds the principles of justice. Consequently, Aquinas affirms multiple moral precepts demanding that all people be treated in appropriate ways. However, his view does explain why human beings tend to stick with family members through thick and thin, while other friendships, even deep ones, often lack the stability and permanency marking familial relationships.

We find the strongest pure natural union between parent and child. The chief relation Aquinas considers is between father and son versus mother and child or simply parent and child. To offer a brief excursus on Aquinas's view of women, his view of women as inferior to men more than anything else clearly influences both this instance of treating father and son versus parent and child, as well as certain aspects of his views on marriage. While a good case can be made that in some key respects Aquinas advances the cause of the equality of women, I take the line that his view on female inferiority is problematic.[3] However, I see no essential connection between his views on love and his notion of female inferiority. Thus, we can leave the latter to the side and assume female equality without injustice to Aquinas's overall account of union and love. His perceptive and

---

2. Aquinas, *Commentary on the Letters of Saint Paul to the Galatians*, 364.
3. For instance, Rose Mary Hayden Lemmons offers the following line of argument: "In other words, even though the science of the day held that femininity results from defective masculinity, Aquinas argues that since the perfection of nature requires females, women are as necessary as men for the perfection of the human species. In this way, Aquinas finds a basis for sexual equality despite the leading scientific viewpoint of his age"; Lemmons, *Ultimate Normative Foundations: The Case for Aquinas's Personalist Natural Law* (Lanham, Md.: Lexington, 2011), 376.

helpful analysis of love should not be the proverbial baby thrown out with the bathwater. What all of this means, practically speaking, is that I am going to present his views on father/son simply in terms of parent/child.[4]

To answer the question of whether parents should love their children more than their own parents, Aquinas again appeals the distinction between the object of love and the power or subject of love. Again, this latter perspective looks at love from the point of view of the lover himself. Regarding the perspective of object loved, he maintains that the one ought to love one's parents more as principle. They are the proximate source of one's existence, nourishment, and education. Consequently, they have a closer analogy to God as the ultimate cause of one's being versus one's relation to one's own children. A person could not exist without his parents, though he could exist without his children. Due to this, a person's love for his parents should involve a filial piety and honor that is not part of his love for his children.

With respect to the second perspective of love taken from the point of the view of the agent as lover, Aquinas holds that human beings naturally do and ought to love their children more than their own parents. He begins with the previously cited principle that "the union arising from natural origin is prior to, and more stable than, all others, because it is something affecting the very substance," and specifies it even further.

In this respect a man loves more that which is more closely connected to him, in which way a man's children are more lovable to him than his father.... First, because parents love their children as being part of themselves, whereas the father is not part of his son, so that the love of a father for his children, is more like a man's love for himself.... Thirdly, because

---

4. In *ST* II-II, q. 26, a. 10, Aquinas asks whether a man ought to love his mother more than his father. He argues a person should not. Even though both are principles of generation, "the father is principle in a more excellent way than the mother, because he is the active principle, while the mother is the passive and material principle." Again, in addition to what has been said previously, Aquinas's view here clearly depends not on philosophical principles but rather on bad science.

children are nearer to their parents, as being part of them, than their parents are to them to whom they stand in a relation of a principle.[5]

The union from natural origin pertains to one's kin broadly construed. Just as the union of similitude drawn from natural origin, in principle, leads to greater love, so, a fortiori, the even greater similitude of parent to child encourages an even stronger and more stable and permanent love. Clearly, such a similitude runs both ways to a high degree. However, Aquinas insists that it runs strongest from parent to child. The reason for this is a metaphysical one: there is not merely a union deriving from natural origin; the child represents a quasi-extension of the parent's own substantial unity.

I say "quasi-extension" because substantial unity cannot literally be shared or extended, as this would violate the principle of *unum* or individuality discussed in chapter 1. Nonetheless, Aquinas uses strong metaphysical language to communicate just how close the union of similitude is between parent and child. This is also why Aquinas mentions "a man's love for himself" in this context. Just as the child is an extension of the parents' own substantial unity, so the parents' love for the child is a fundamental extension of their own love of self.

This entails that all of the properties of friendship that have their origin in the ways that a person relates to oneself in the love of self have a heightened intensity in relation to a parents' love for a child over other friendships. In terms of the property of longing, which in the case of self-love includes the desire for self-preservation, parents show a greater willingness to lay down their lives for their children more than for any other persons (with the possible exception of marriage, which we will treat subsequently). In terms of benevolence, parents simply have a greater desire to see their children flourish relative to analogous desires for other kids—even nieces and nephews among their larger kin. In terms of beneficence, parents do more for their children than others—this includes making

---

5. *ST* II-II, q. 26, a. 9.

great sacrifices of time, effort, and resources to foster the well-being of their children. Parents enjoy, or at least desire to enjoy, the presence of their kids in a singular way and derive great delight from their children's accomplishments. Last, parents seek to effect concord between them and their kids in a unique way through familial obedience. Children are to desire and seek the same sorts of things as their parents by way of conforming their wills to them out of filial reverence. Much more should be said on Aquinas's account of reverence and obedience. We will do so in chapter 5, as it ties into the role of the love of God, which we have yet to address directly. To summarize the discussion for our present purposes, the unique union of similitude of parent to child effects an intense and active love aimed at fostering and sustaining a real loving union with the children.

To apply the principal point addressed in chapter 1 concerning the relation between the love of self and the love of others, proper self-love best positions parents to achieve the desired real union with their children. Of particular importance to this context is the necessity of proper versus wicked self-love. Parents marked by disordered self-love, in all but the worst cases, will still perceive their children to be an extension of themselves in a real way. Accordingly, they will love their children, but much of what they will to their children will reflect the lack of a proper frame of reference for what is fully good, due to the inability to will such things first to themselves. Persons can give only what they have, and they will tend to give others the "goods" they habitually will to themselves. Nonetheless, even this case illustrates the explanatory power of Aquinas's account. Individuals with disordered interior lives tend not to be reliable friends. However, when it comes to their own children, they make the best effort they can to sustain and nurture their union with them. The high degree of similitude naturally inclines parents to do so, whether or not the orientation of their own self-love allows for the achievement of the real union desired.

Conversely, parents marked by proper self-love are much more likely to seek and obtain true goods for their children. Moreover, parents will be less likely to reduce their children to mere means for their own interests and happiness insofar as their love for their children will be the love of friendship versus the love of concupiscence—they will love their children for the children's own sake. Last, the proper love of self, for reasons we will address in chapter 5, leads to the most sustainable self-governance and consistent love on behalf of one's friends or, in this case, one's own children. The proximity of children to each parent's own unity inclines parents to great love. However, the possibility of acting on that inclination to develop a deep love still depends upon the condition of one's love of self. Even in the context of one's own children, self-love has priority over the love of others.

THE EQUALIZING EFFECT OF CHARITY

While Aquinas affirms the universality of natural love in several passages, he also has great concerns about the deformation of natural love through sin and the strict necessity of grace for its restoration. For instance, he occasionally makes comments like the following:

> There is a love which springs from charity, and another which is worldly. This worldly love does not include everyone, because we love those with whom there is some communication or sharing, which is the cause of love; but in worldly love this cause is not present in everyone, but is only found in one's relatives or other worldly people. But the love of charity does extend to everyone.[6]

Regardless of Aquinas's full explanation of the status of natural love in light of sin, what is clear is the role charity performs in the restoration and transformation of it. Charity plays the key role in Aquinas's overall ethical account as that which unifies all other virtues and cements a person's loving real union with God. Accordingly, we will address it in much greater detail when we turn to love in rela-

---

6. Aquinas, *Commentary on the Letter of Saint Paul to the Colossians*, trans. Fr. Fabian R. Larcher, OP, B. Mortensen, and D. Keating, ed. J. Mortensen and E. Alarcon (Lander, Wyo.: Aquinas Institute for the Study of Sacred Doctrine, 2012), 11.

tion to God in the next chapter. However, Aquinas employs charity in the current context of similitude to make the point of universality. So, I want to offer a brief overview of the virtue of charity here to show how it applies to the extension of love.

Aquinas defines charity as the infused virtue that makes a person a friend with God. Individuals are to love other human beings out of charity insofar as all human beings are related to God. Aquinas uses the analogy of human friendship to illustrate charity's structure. Being a friend to someone involves concord—willing and desiring the same fundamental sorts of things. Thus, a lover has a love for the children of a beloved more than children of nonfriends. He loves his friends' children because his friends love their own children. Similarly, because the principal object of charity is God, and its principal act is uniting oneself to God in love, the more one loves God, the more one loves other human beings. God's "children," in this case, are all human beings. Each human being is a creature of God. In turn, God loves each creature, and even more the personal creatures. This is why and how the charitable love of God extends to the love of neighbor. As every person constitutes a neighbor in this sense, the charitable love of others is a universal love. Aquinas speaks to the literalness of loving all human beings in terms of the love of one's enemies. God loves one's enemies, and thus one should love one's own enemies.

In previously cited passages in which Aquinas speaks to the varying intensity of love appropriate to the degree of similitude present, he also affirms the equality of love in terms of its object. For instance, in the passage from his *Commentary on Galatians*, he states:

> It should be noted that love can be called greater or less in two ways. In one way, from the standpoint of the object; in another, from the intensity of the act.... Therefore, with respect to the first [standpoint], we ought to love everyone equally, because we ought to wish the good of eternal life to everyone.[7]

---

7. Aquinas, *Commentary on the Letters of Saint Paul to the Galatians*, 364.

Charity builds upon and perfects nature. Natural love as based on similitude naturally admits of degrees in proportion to the level of similitude. Thereby, charity also admits of degrees.

While charity admits of degrees, willing the good to all others forms its baseline act in relation to other human beings. Due to this, charity serves to correct a possible and likely exaggeration within natural love—namely, loving only those with whom one has a high degree of similitude. The natural tendency of the love of self is to will goods to others, because a person recognizes if he desires such things as good for him, then he, out of proper self-love, should will those same goods to any being with the same nature. While this natural tendency extends outward, there remains a distinct possibility of a subtler form of selfishness, whereby one loves only those with whom he perceives an immediate similitude. Charity reinforces the fact that he has the same nature as all other human creatures of God. Since, through charity, he sees that a loving union with God constitutes the greatest good, then he, through consistency, should will that same good to others. In this way, charity counters even this form of selfishness.

Again, Aquinas thinks that, even at the natural level, principles of justice exclude treating groups of people in various harmful and selfish ways, and the similitude of human nature allows for the possibility of friendly relations among everyone. "This is evident when a man loses his way; for everyone stops even an unknown stranger from taking the wrong road, as if every man is naturally a familiar and a friend of every other man."[8] Nonetheless, the sinful inclinations toward distrust and selfishness can cause people to use differences as a reason to exclude others in morally deficient ways. Charity combats this tendency at the supernatural level, particularly at the limit with its requirement that even those perceived or actual enemies must be loved.

---

8. Aquinas, *Commentary on Aristotle's Nicomachean Ethics*, 1541.

MARRIAGE AS THE GREATEST HUMAN UNION

In general terms, Aquinas's principle states that the greater the similitude, the greater the stability and permanency of the love. The greater the permanency of the love, the greater real union the lovers seek and likely obtain. Thus, a greater similitude prima facie effects a greater real union between friends. The ultimate rationale for this principle draws from the relation between unity and union. As unity is the principle of union, the closer two things are together naturally, the closer they can be through love. At the level of persons, the closer a relationship with another person comes to unity, the stronger it will be. Since self-love arises immediately from substantial unity, we can say that the more a lover's love for the beloved approaches one's own self-love (and vice versa), the greater the loving union between them will be. In other words, the most stable and permanent love relationship will be the one that approximates most each person's love of self. Moreover, friendships based on choice often effect a greater intensity of love relative to friendships based on nature. Marriage forms a union with the potential for the greatest stability and permanency based on nature and the greatest intensity based on choice. In short, marriage forms the greatest human union *simpliciter*.

In the continuing discussion of the order of charity, subsequent to the question on whether parents ought to love their children more than their own parents, Aquinas asks "whether a man ought to love his wife more than his father and mother." His primary response draws upon the distinction between object and union. A husband should love his parents more from the perspective of object, as the principle for his existence. In contrast to this, a man should love his wife more intensely due to the union possessed with her. Responding to an objection citing St. Paul's words that a husband should "love his wife as himself," Aquinas clarifies:

The words of the Apostle do not mean that a man ought to love his wife equally with himself, but that a man's love for himself is the reason for his love of his wife, since she is one with him.⁹

The love of self is the root and form of the love of others. The more the beloved approximates the lover's own self-love, the greater love the lover has for the beloved. To put the point in terms of unity, the more the beloved approximates the lover's own unity, the greater the union possible between them. On account of this, for Aquinas, marriage represents the highest form of union between two persons, and this in light of all three unions of love.

In the *Summa contra Gentiles*, Aquinas states that "there seems to be the greatest friendship between husband and wife."¹⁰ Given his overall account of marriage, I think he means this proposition literally. The greatest friendship possible between human beings is marriage (as we will discuss in the next chapter, the greatest friendship possible *simpliciter* is with God). This is due to the metaphysical relationship between unity and union and love's dependency upon that relationship. Marriage allows for the greater friendship due in large part to the decisive role indissolubility performs within it. Let us begin with a look at his general account of marriage.¹¹

---

9. *ST* II-II, q. 26, a. 11, ad 2.

10. Aquinas, *Summa contra Gentiles*, trans. Vernon J. Bourke (Notre Dame, Ind.: University of Notre Dame Press, 1975), III, c. 123, p. 6.

11. I think Aquinas's account of marriage suffers from the previously discussed notion that women are naturally inferior to men. As mentioned then, I reject this notion and do not see an essential dependency of his view of love to it. In either case, my interpretation of Aquinas's view on marriage presented here does not extend to this aspect of his thought. Interestingly, Colleen McCluskey makes the case that if Aquinas were consistent, he would have recognized that there is an essential dependency, but it runs the other way. In this case, his view of conjugal love entails a straightforward equality of man and woman. She states, "It is a pity that Aquinas himself did not recognize the implications of his own theory, for it would have enabled him to challenge the many inequalities that women of his own time faced"; McCluskey, "An Unequal Relationship between Equals: Thomas Aquinas on Marriage," *History of Philosophy Quarterly* 24, no. 1 (January 2007): 14. Peter Kwasniewski criticizes her analysis as reductionist, arguing that she and other "modern commentators tend to be blinded by a preoccupation with his purported sexism and thereby fail to see the nobility of his conception of spousal love, which is apparent only when one adopts a properly *theological* hermeneutic";

He argues that matrimony is a natural state for human beings. The most basic implication of the status "natural" is that marriage is not sinful. More directly and importantly, such status entails that marriage is a good for human nature and the human individual; it is something that, in principle, contributes to virtue and flourishing. For his primary argument for the goodness of marriage in this context, he draws from the nature of human procreation and care of offspring. Raising children requires significant time and resources. A lasting, healthy relationship between the parents best promotes this end of rearing flourishing children.

What makes marriage unique among human friendships is its voluntary indissolubility. Addressing this notion, Aquinas states the following:

> Furthermore, the greater that friendship is, the more solid and long-lasting will it be. Now, there seems to be the greatest friendship between husband and wife, for they are united not only in the act of fleshly union, which produces gentle association even among beasts, but also in partnership of the whole range of domestic activity. Consequently, as an indication of this, man must even "leave his father and mother" for the sake of his wife, as is said in Genesis (2:24). Therefore, it is fitting for matrimony to be completely indissoluble (*indissolubile*).[12]

As we saw in chapter 2, the natural union of similitude between countrymen and colleagues and, ultimately, between parent and child allows for increasingly strong relationships. The similitude in these cases is purely natural—the similitude is present whether willed or not. Aquinas holds that friendships grounded in a high degree of similitude possess a natural stability and permanency, but friendships arising from choice can be more intense due to what unites the friends. The marital oath creates a unique intensity insofar as it creates the greatest similitude possible—the spouses each choose to identify with the other as an extension of themselves. The two

---

Kwasniewski, "St. Thomas on the Grandeur and Limitations of Marriage," *Nova et Vetera* 10, no. 2 (2012): 422n43.

12. *ScG* III, c. 123, p. 6.

become one with respect to the one flesh effected by sexual union, engaging in "the whole range of domestic activity," and in the real union of their inner lives.

Aquinas analyzes the implication of an indissoluble friendship. In this context, he contends that marriage's status as a friendship forms a strong reason against having multiple spouses. Friendship presupposes equality between the friends. If a man had several wives, "it would not be lawful ... for the friendship of wife for husband would not be free, but somewhat servile."[13] Moreover, strong, intimate friendships are possible only with a few people. "Therefore, if a wife has but one husband, but the husband has several wives, the friendship will not be equal on both sides. So, the friendship will not be free, but servile in some way."[14] From considerations of both equality and the relative exclusivity of complete friendships, Aquinas concludes that marriage ought to be between two and only two people. Any other arrangement violates the nature of friendship and leaves at least one of the spouses disadvantaged.

Within the marital union, we find the potential for the highest realization of love's inner-tendency toward unity between two separate persons.

> As to be one is better than to be united, so there is more oneness in love which is directed to self than in love which unites one to others. Dionysius used the terms *uniting* and *binding* in order to show the derivation of love from self to things outside self; as uniting is derived from unity.[15]

In any love of friendship, the lover seeks a real union with the beloved. To some degree, a person wants the experience of unity or oneness that he has with himself with the beloved in friendship. As we saw in the previous chapter, provided the lover and beloved both have proper self-love, they can enter into an intimate union of shared interior lives making "one heart of two."

Marriage as a kind of friendship possesses all of the characteris-

---

13. *ScG* III, c. 124, p. 4.
14. *ScG* III, c. 124, p. 5.
15. *ST* I q. 60, a. 3, ad 2.

tics of friendship: longing, ecstasy, mutual indwelling, conversation, benevolence, beneficence, pleasure, and concord. Additionally, insofar as Aquinas construes marriage as the greatest of friendships, we should expect some further characteristics or at least a heightened mode of possessing the characteristics. We find both in marriage. Willed indissolubility or indivisibility distinguishes marriage from every other kind of loving union. Indissolubility, in turn, serves to intensify the other aspects of friendship. It is the one thing that allows for the union of mutual possession to approximate in the greatest way possible the substantial unity undergirding self-love and allowing for the full actualization of interior personal life found in proper self-love.

Since self-love is based on substantial oneness, there exists a continual conjunction of the union of similitude and the union of possession. The metaphysical inseparability of these two unions creates the conditions for the depth and vitality found in proper self-love. No relationship between two persons can achieve the same unity due to the merely contingent conjunction of the unions of similitude and possession. However, indissolubility performs the role in marriage that metaphysical inseparability plays in proper self-love. It creates the framework and foundation for the natural dynamism of proper self-love of willing and acquiring appropriate goods for oneself to extend and be united to the beloved. The love of affection, safeguarded by the merging of similitudes into one via indissolubility, is fully free and unrestrained to effect a real union of inner lives. This complete co-union creates at the positive limit a shared life, a communion of two metaphysically distinct persons habitually mutually indwelling with each other with full intimacy, sharing, trust, delight, and concord.

By comparison, in the case of nonspousal friends who are friends by choice (versus kinship and natural similitude), the love of friendship still effects a real union of inner lives. Moreover, the friends might lead shared lives marked by intensity. The sharing and intensity, though, depend upon the stability of the mutual choice of each person. If either friend chooses otherwise, the friendship ceases to be. Thus, in these kinds of friendships, the possibility of voluntary separation inevitably colors and limits the depth of the union and the experience of the marks of friendship. Similarly, in friendships between kin, nature strongly encourages the friendship, but it is still dependent upon the continued willingness to be friends.

The loving union between parent and child comes closest to the union of marriage. Thus, it is the second most intimate human relationship possible. However, it must rank second for Aquinas because of the metaphysical asymmetry built into it. To restate Aquinas's key claim in this regard, "Because parents love their children as being part of themselves, whereas the father is not part of his son, so that the love of a father for his children, is more like a man's love for himself." Children have a strong metaphysical likeness to their parents. Parents rightly view their child as a part of themselves. However, the child does not view his parents as part of himself. Like marriage, the parent/child relationship does, by nature, extend until death, but such filial friendships are not between equals. Thereby, they cannot reach the same level of intimacy as spousal love.

In marriage, we have a friendship of equals whose only limiting characteristic is death. Therefore, when it is said that through marriage "the two become one," Aquinas suggests that this is not purely metaphorical. The union of marriage comes as close to metaphysical oneness or unity as possible. Marital union, or the union of possession obtained through the mark of indissolubility, encompasses sexual union, the union of cooperation in the raising of children, and, most generally, the union of interior lives fully shared by one another. These are the reasons that, for Aquinas, marriage is the greatest of friendships.

It should be noted that, while indissolubility is a necessary structural condition for marriage as the greatest possible friendship, it is obviously not sufficient. The other key component, as we saw in relation to any healthy complete friendship, is proper self-love on the part of both individuals. There are two reasons for this. The first concerns the vital role healthy self-love plays in willing goods to others. A person wills and seeks goods to others as he wills them to himself. In the case of any attempt at a friendship, if a lover is not accustomed or knowledgeable in the practice of seeking real goods, he will not be in position to will such things to another. The second reason concerns what the lover offers to the beloved in terms of shared lives. The lover must share his interior life with the beloved, but only if that interior life is appropriately ordered though proper self-love will it be the sort of thing worth sharing. At the limit, we could explain this in terms of marriage as a gift of self. What I mean by this is that, if a lover expects the beloved to receive himself as a good, then the lover is rationally committed to thinking of himself as a good worth giving and sharing. In turn, being good, when it comes to human beings, requires a proper love of self, doing and seeking those things contributing to the full actualization and perfection of oneself.

Michael Waldstein offers a compelling comparative analysis of Aquinas and Karol Wojtyla on the notion of giving of oneself in love. I think he is effective in showing the reasonableness of holding that Aquinas includes this element in his understanding of friendship.[16] Waldstein cites Aquinas's *Commentary on John* to flesh out what is entailed in the full realization of the property of ecstasy or going outside of oneself. His translation of Aquinas reads as follows:

> Love is twofold, namely, love of friendship and love of concupiscence, but they differ. In the love of concupiscence we draw to ourselves what is outside of us when by that very love we love things other than ourselves inasmuch as they are useful or delightful to us. In the love of friendship, on the other hand, it is the other way around, because we draw ourselves to what is outside. For, to those whom we love in that love we are related to as ourselves, *communicating ourselves to them in some way*.[17]

Through an act of communicating or sharing oneself to or with the other, Waldstein contends a person gives of himself or makes him-

---

16. Michael Waldstein, "John Paul II and St. Thomas on Love and the Trinity (first and second part)," *Anthropotes* 18 (2002): 113–38 and 269–86.

17. Aquinas, *Commentary on the Gospel of John*, 2036; Waldstein, "John Paul II and St. Thomas on Love and the Trinity," 129.

self a gift for the beloved. Such sharing or communicating, when mutual and reciprocal, culminates in interpersonal communion. He notes that this dimension pertains to any complete friendship, but has a special realization in spousal love.

St. Thomas seems to state a general rule that applies not only to God, but to love in general: "To give oneself is an indication of great love." It must be granted that some kinds of friendship primarily involve cooperation in a common work and sharing in a common good rather than the enjoyment of one another as a concupiscible good. Such enjoyment of one another as a good is clearest in spousal love. Still, a certain self-communication, St. Thomas claims, is an essential aspect of the love of friendship in general. It follows that, when this love is mutually known and accepted, and when a shared life is built up, one can speak of a gift of self in some sense in all friendships. In giving the gift of himself through the love of friendship each friend becomes for the other a good to be enjoyed.[18]

The notion of a complete gift of self ties into the shared life and merging of unities (to the degree possible) made possible in marriage. Since each spouse shares to the highest degree possible what it is to be his unique self to the other, they create the closest union possible between them. Again, the strict unity of selfhood prevents a union in which the two unities would be lost or altogether merged. Marital union can only approximate unity.

In terms of a more practical role the love of self performs in the gift of self, it would be odd to consider himself a good thing to give or communicate to someone else if a person does not apprehend his goodness and love himself. As we showed in chapter 1 and will expand upon in chapters 4 and 5, this is not to say a person should be self-absorbed. Quite the opposite. All people possess common self-love and lovingly relate to themselves in terms of what they think they are. However, self-love becomes proper only when directed toward that which most directly makes one a person—namely, a concrete and unique substance of a rational nature and all the goods ap-

---

18. Waldstein, "John Paul II and St. Thomas," 131. The included citation is from Aquinas, *Commentary on the Gospel of John*, 480.

propriate to such a being. Otherwise, common self-love degenerates into wicked or disordered self-love, leading to a miserable interior life and inability to relate properly to others. Thus, wicked self-love creates a double roadblock to a successful marriage as friendship.

First, a wicked person does not know how to relate to others in love, since he cannot even relate to himself properly. Second, a person would not know how to respond well to the beloved who wishes to give of herself in love. Such a person would not know how to receive the gift of self of the other. In light of such a person's improper self-love, he would only be able to relate to the other as he does to himself. He could love the corporeal nature of the other in a love of concupiscence, but he could not love or receive the full personhood of the beloved with a love of friendship. This limitation would be most pronounced in the inability to accept the fullness of the interior life of the other persons.

To conclude, indissolubility serves to create the potential for the most intense and sustained loving relationship between two human beings—a fully shared existence and stable mutual indwelling. With the potential for a great good comes the potential for a privation of that good. It is, perhaps, unsurprising that when marriages go bad, we often witness an unmatched mutual hatred and spite between two persons relative to any other kinds of falling out people might have. This misery and discord between the spouses approximates the full miserable experience of oneself in wicked or disordered self-love—a notion we will expand upon in chapter 4. This real possibility reinforces the necessity of cultivating what needs to be cultivated to allow the marital union to flourish. In this context, a key, if not *the* key, is proper self-love. Appropriately developed spousal love depends upon both proper self-giving to the beloved and proper receiving of the beloved, and both proper self-giving and proper receiving depend upon proper self-love.

3

Participation and the Love of God

THE LOVE OF SELF AND
THE LOVE OF GOD

Aquinas characterizes charity as the infused virtue by which human beings are united to God in friendship. Moreover, this same virtue serves to unify the ethical life insofar as it "directs the acts of all other virtues to the last end."[1] A loving union with God forms the ultimate end of human life. In the context of the loving friendship of charity, Aquinas asks "whether, out of charity, man is bound to love God more than himself."[2]

This question might seem superfluous, as the entire Judeo-Christian tradition affirms the love of God above all else, even one's own self. However, it is a necessary question for Aquinas to ask and address, given his principles that we have already examined. Union derives from unity. Unity is the metaphysical basis for the love of self, and that love must be greater than love of others. The highest union possible between two human beings is one that still falls short of substantial unity. If human beings do not share a unity with God, it would seem that the best one could hope for is an intimate union with God that is even closer than the union obtainable in the best

---

1. *ST* II-II, q. 23, a. 8.
2. *ST* II-II, q. 26, a. 3.

Participation and the Love of God 45

marriage. The problem, then, would be that the metaphysics of the situation would entail that, based on natural principles, one's love of self must exceed the love he has for God.

Perhaps, then, Aquinas could simply say that charity as an infused virtue overcomes these natural principles. On this hypothesis, grace will not be thwarted by metaphysics or nature and itself creates the conditions for a greater love of God over self against nature. However, Aquinas never makes this move on any point regarding the relationship between nature and grace. Grace does not overcome nature; rather, it builds upon and perfects it. On his actual view, charity demands the greater love of God over self in part because nature allows for the same.

> The good we receive from God is twofold, the good of nature, and the good of grace. Now the fellowship of natural goods bestowed on us by God is the foundation of natural love, in virtue of which not only man, so long as his nature remains unimpaired, loves God above all things and more than himself.[3]

Continuing in the next article, Aquinas elaborates:

> God is loved as the principle of good, on which the love of charity is founded; while man, out of charity, loves himself by reason of his being a partaker of the aforesaid good, and loves his neighbor by reason of his fellowship in that good. Now fellowship is a reason for love according to a certain union in relation to God. Wherefore just as unity surpasses union, the fact that man himself has a share of the Divine good, is a more potent reason for loving than that another should be a partner with him in that share.[4]

Aquinas retains and reemphasizes the natural principles of love in the context of charity. A person is capable of loving God more than

---

3. Ibid.
4. *ST* II-II, q. 26, a. 4. Also in *ST* I-II, q. 109, a. 3, *sed contra*, Aquinas affirms, "As some maintain, man was first made with only natural endowments; and in this state it is manifest that he loved God to some extent. But he did not love God equally with himself, or less than himself, otherwise he would have sinned. Therefore he loved God above himself. Therefore man, by his natural powers alone, can love God more than himself and above all things."

self even at the natural level due to a metaphysical connection to God as the principle of good.

Aquinas employs his understanding of metaphysical participation to explain the priority of the love of God over the love of self.[5] He characterizes participation as follows: "When something receives in a particular way that which belongs to another in a universal way, it is said 'to participate' in that."[6] Hence, participation conveys the idea of being connected in a fundamental metaphysical manner to the thing in which one participates. At the most basic level, each being's act of existence participates in God as cause.

In his discussion of the connections between self-love and loving others, Gallagher shows that for Aquinas the basis for loving God is not the union of similitude, but the relation of part to whole. Any part is ordered or inclined toward the good of the whole, as an individual person is ordered to the common good. The part/whole dynamic takes on a different character in relation to God. He employs Aquinas's principle found in *De Divinis Nominbus*: "What is superior among beings is compared to what is inferior as a whole to part, insofar as the superior has perfectly and completely what the inferior has imperfectly and particularly."[7]

When Thomas treats the relation of the creature to God as one of part to whole, he does so not in a pantheistic way such that all creatures would be parts of God, but rather in terms of his doctrine of participation, by which each creature has in a partial form perfections that are found in their complete or perfect form only in God. Whatever goodness they have in themselves and find lovable in themselves is to be found in a full, more perfect form in God.[8]

---

5. I am indebted to John W. Wippel's analysis of participation in *The Metaphysical Thought of Thomas Aquinas: From Finite Being to Uncreated Being* (Washington, D.C.: The Catholic University of America Press, 2000).

6. Aquinas, *The Exposition of the "On the Hebdomads" of Boethius*, trans. Janice L. Schultz and Edward A. Synan (Washington, D.C.: The Catholic University of America Press, 2001), lect. 2, p. 70.

7. Aquinas, *De Divinis Nominbus*, 4.9, n. 406, as quoted in Gallagher, "Desire for Beatitude and Love of Friendship in Thomas Aquinas," *Medieval Studies* 58 (1996): 36.

8. Gallagher, "Thomas Aquinas on Self-Love as the Basis of Love of Others," 36. See also Patrick Lee, "St. Thomas on Love of Self and Love of Others," in *The Renewal of*

Each human being participates in or is so deeply metaphysically connected to God that his fundamental orientation is to him as the proper source of one's own goodness.

Thomas Osborne offers the following helpful reconstruction of Aquinas's basic argument concerning such participation:

1. Every single thing loves that according to which it is designed by nature. (assumption)

2. The good of the part is on account of the good of the whole. (assumption)

3. The part is designed by nature for the good of the whole. (corollary of 2)

4. Every part loves the good of the whole more than its own good. (by 1, 3)

5. Every creature is a part of the universe. (implicit assumption)

6. Every single thing by natural appetite loves its own good on account of the good of the whole universe. (by 4, 5)

7. The good of the whole universe is God. (assumption)

8. In his integral state a human a naturally loves God more than himself. (by 6, 7)[9]

Every creature, while metaphysically distinct from God, participates in his goodness and perfection. By nature, each person loves God more than self, in part, because he seeks the full actualization of his unity, which must refer to the whole, perfect good. Moreover, the "whole good" necessarily refers to God as the ultimate source and realization of perfection. While the wounds of fallen nature have undermined this naturally superior love of God, the grace of charity restores the possibility.[10] Thus, grace does not replace or act contrary

---

Civilization: Essays in Honor of Jacques Maritain, ed. Gavin T. Colvert (Washington, D.C.: The Catholic University of America Press, 2010), 242.

9. Thomas M. Osborne Jr., *Love of Self and Love of God in Thirteenth-Century Ethics* (Notre Dame, Ind.: University of Notre Dame Press, 2005), 78.

10. In connection to *ST* I, q. 60, a. 5, Osborne notes, "If a human's nature were integral, he would be able to love God more than himself even out of his own natural powers. This ability to so love God is based on the natural inclination planted in him by God. It is

to natural principles; rather, it first restores those principles and then builds upon them. As we will see with Aquinas's characterization of God as the prime mover of will, sin has not thoroughly destroyed the natural principles. Rather, it has only hindered them.

In comparing the love of God to the love of other human beings, in the case of one person loving another human person, the union of similitude between the two persons creates the condition for mutual affection and the desire for real union. In the case of a person's love of God, due to the difference in kind between God and man, the union of similitude does not entirely account for how a person can love God more than self. Human beings, as made in the image and likeness of God, do possess a certain similitude with him. However, the similitude does not run both ways. "For, we say that a statue is like a man, but not conversely; so also a creature can be spoken of as in some sort like God; but not that God is like a creature."[11] Moreover, similitude with God would, at best, make possible an equal love of God and self. Thus, similitude cannot account for the greater love of God over self.

Instead of appealing to similitude, Aquinas explains the greater love by way of participation in God. I contend that we can draw the following conclusion from these considerations: a person is metaphysically united to God in such a way that renders substantial unity an inherently relational kind of thing—what it is to be a created unity is to be a being whose very oneness constitutively relates to God. This is the case due to Aquinas's affirmation of three principles: first, unity is greater than union as principle to principled; second, unity is a cause of greater love than union; third, a person can and should love God more than himself.

These three principles entail one of two options: first, there exists a metaphysical unity of God and each human being; or second,

---

only because of the weakness of fallen nature that this purely natural love is now impossible without grace. The natural inclination of the will towards God shows that the natural elective love of God is possible"; Osborne, *Love of Self*, 108.

11. *ST* I, q. 4, a. 3, ad 4.

the weaker option, a person's metaphysical relation to God constitutes something so fundamental that his very unity and identity have an ongoing relational dependency in God. Aquinas's disavowal of pantheism rules out the first option.[12] In terms of participation, Aquinas avoids pantheism by distinguishing God's necessary existence from the finite existence of created being. As John Wippel notes, commenting on *Quodlibet* 2, q. 2, a.1, "Being (*ens*) is predicated of God alone essentially, and of every creature only by participation; for no creature is its *esse*, but merely has *esse*."[13]

We are left, then, with the second option: the metaphysical connection of participation of each creature to God establishes a necessary metaphysical relational identity to God. To be an individual, a being who is one/*unum*, is to be related to God as that in which one participates. In the context of human beings, a person does not and cannot exist as an isolated unity, but as a unity deriving its very act of being from an ongoing participation in God himself. Moreover, this fact accounts for the possibility of the greater love of God over self.[14] While sin has marred the human person's natural tendency to affective and real union with God, the metaphysical foundation remains, while grace restores and elevates nature and the desire for God.

The next section will look at how the love of self properly relates to the love of God, particularly in terms of two conditions. The first condition is that the love of God more than self is necessary for proper self-love. The second condition is that the love of God does not threaten the proper love of self. Stump neatly summarizes the constructive versus competitive relation between the two kinds of love entailed in Aquinas's view.

---

12. *ST* I, q. 3, a. 8.

13. Wippel, *Metaphysical Thought of Thomas Aquinas*, 105.

14. In his overview of medieval philosophy, Étienne Gilson explains the connection of the love of any good to the love of God in the following way: "It is impossible to love the image without at the same time loving the original. What holds of the whole totality of creatures holds much more of man in particular. To will any object is to will an image of God, that is, to will God; to love oneself, then, will be to love an analogue of God, and that is to love God"; Gilson, *The Spirit of Mediaeval Philosophy* (Notre Dame, Ind.: University of Notre Dame Press, 1991), 286.

On Aquinas's views, for every person, internal integration is necessary for the real good for that person, and the ultimate real good is union with God.... So, on Aquinas's account, love of oneself is in fact necessary for any love of another, including God. A perfect love of God, therefore, cannot compete with the love of oneself. A perfect love of God *requires* love of oneself.[15]

A person cannot love God without self-love, but the love of God ought always to be greater than one's love of self.

THE NATURAL INCLINATION TO THE LOVE OF GOD

Just as the relation between unity and union forms the basis and parameters for the possible love between human beings, so the metaphysical relation between God and human beings in terms of whole and part determines the structure of love between God and human beings. Aquinas holds that God wills two basic things, "Himself to be, and other things to be; but Himself as the end, and other things as ordained to that end."[16] Insofar as God wills, he loves, as love is the proper act of the will. Thus, God loves himself and all else that exists. The term of the latter love is God himself.

Responding to the objection that love cannot exist in God because he is simple and love is a uniting and binding force, Aquinas states:

An act of love always tends towards two things; to the good that one wills, and to the person for whom one wills it: since to love a person is to wish that person good. Hence, inasmuch as we love ourselves, we wish ourselves good; and, so far as possible, union with that good.... And by the fact that anyone loves another, he wills good to that other. Thus he puts the other, as it were, in the place of himself. So far love is a binding force, since it aggregates another to ourselves, and refers his good to our own. And then again the divine love is a binding force, inasmuch as God wills good to others.[17]

---

15. Stump, *Wandering in Darkness*, 101–2.
16. *ST* I, q. 19, a. 2.
17. *ST* I, q. 20, a. 1, ad 3.

God wills the good to each creature, in particular each rational creature, and thereby loves them. God's love of each thing constitutes an act of drawing that thing to himself. Moreover, since God neither needs creatures, nor can creatures add to his beatitude, the love by which he loves all things cannot be the love of concupiscence. God loves human beings necessarily with a love of friendship. God wills the good of himself to each person, and God wills himself to each person for his own sake.

From the perspective of the response to this love by human beings, just as the relation between unity and union naturally inclines people to enter into loving relationships with one another, so the relation between participation in God and unity inclines persons to enter into a loving union with God. For Aquinas, while this love achieves its perfection on the supernatural level, it begins at the natural level. The most basic way that human beings experience this inclination to love is through the fundamental impulse of the will.

Aquinas affirms that God is the exterior principle by which the will is moved insofar as the universal good is the cause of the will. Each and every particular good derives its goodness from participation in the universal good.

> God moves man's will, as the Universal Mover, to the universal object of the will, which is good. And without this universal motion, man cannot will anything. But man determines himself by his reason to will this or that.[18]

Of course, a person may not and need not realize that the universal good is God, as this recognition ranges from implicit to explicit. The most proper form of knowledge of good is the knowledge of God.

> All things, by desiring their own perfection, desire God Himself, inasmuch as the perfections of all things are so many similitudes of the divine being.... And so of those things which desire God, some know Him as He is Himself, and this is proper to the rational creatures.[19]

---

18. *ST* I-II, q. 9, a. 6, ad 3; see also *ST* I, q. 60, a. 5.
19. *ST* I, q. 6, a. 1, ad 2. Fulvio Di Blasi argues that through the active intellect, a person should come to know the universal good is God; Di Blasi, "Knowledge of the Good as Participation in God's Love," *Giornale di Metafisica* 27, no. 2 (2005): 469–89.

Whether or not a person apprehends God as the whole and perfect good, he nevertheless experiences the pull toward the good. A person's conscious experience includes the fundamental awareness both of one's being as good and of an orientation toward the acquisition of further goods for oneself and, by extension, one's neighbors. "Now that which, first and foremost, is most natural to man, is the love of what is good, and especially the love of the Divine good, and of his neighbor's good."[20]

Aquinas's account of such personal experience follows his account of being in general. The act of being is not static but, instead, dynamic and relational. Due to the objective ontological connection of a person's substantial unity to the universal good, a person's experience is colored and shaped by an inclination for good-seeking activity. If a person progresses to apprehend the universal good as God, he becomes aware of God as the center of gravity to which his conscious life is being pulled. Moreover, the pull toward God is not one inclination among many; rather, it is the most fundamental and primal dynamism shaping conscious awareness of goodness.

The term of the pull toward God, based on the natural principles previously stated, involves uniting oneself to God, but the crucial way by which this occurs is not through a full, mutual friendship with God. Rather, natural union occurs through religion, the nonsupernatural virtue by which persons direct themselves to God.

> [Religion] denotes properly a relation to God. For it is He to Whom we ought to be bound as to our unfailing principle; to Whom also our choice should be resolutely directed as to our last end; and Whom we lose when we neglect Him by sin, and should recover by believing in Him and confessing our faith.[21]

Supernatural faith subsumes the natural virtue of religion into an integrated life, but the principles of the latter are distinct from it and natural.

Religion is annexed to the virtue of justice and as such is a virtue

20. *ST* II-II, q. 34, a. 5.
21. *ST* II-II, q. 81, a. 1.

of the will. Any virtue of the will immediately concerns proper love, as love is the chief act of the will itself. A person cultivates good, habitual love by disposing the will toward true goods, and in the context of loving others, willing those goods with the love of friendship. Religion annexes to justice versus being a straightforward species of it for an important reason. Justice, essentially, "consists in rendering to another his due according to equality,"[22] and religion cannot give render to God an equal due.[23] Accordingly, whereby a person can perform a complete act of justice by rendering to another person what is due to that person, he cannot do so with respect to God. Religion, deriving its structure from the metaphysical fact of participation in God as the source of one's own unity, never satisfies what is due to God. Rather, it continually draws a person toward a deeper conscious union with God. The reverence owed to God promotes the proper acts of religion, such as worship, devotion, prayer, and adoration, by which a person unites himself to God as the first principle of his being and his being as good. The virtue of religion cultivates a proper love of God as the first principle of existence.

At times, Aquinas indicates that the union effected by religion is a sort of friendship with God. For instance, in his *Commentary on I Corinthians*, he states:

Now we have a twofold union with God: one refers to the goods of nature, which we partake of here from him; the other refers to beatitude, inasmuch as through grace we partake here of heavenly felicity, as far as possible here.... According to the first communication with God there is

---

22. *ST* II-II, q. 80. On this point, I benefited from reading Kevin E. O'Reilly, OP, "The Significance of Worship in the Thought of Thomas Aquinas: Some Reflections," *International Philosophical Quarterly* 53, no. 4 (2013): 453–62.

23. Aquinas reasons similarly in terms of piety—rendering what is due to one's parents—and observance—rendering what is due to one's homeland. His hierarchical ranking of religion, piety, and observance reflects the degree to which there is an inequality—religion involves the greatest disparity, whereas observance involves the least. For additional considerations of the relatedness among these three virtues, see Paul Cornish, "John Courtney Murray and St. Thomas Aquinas on Obedience and the Civil Conversation," *Vera Lex* 9, nos. 1–2 (2008): 49–75, and Michael P. Krom, "Civic Virtue: Aquinas on Piety, Observance, and Religion," *Proceedings of the American Catholic Philosophical Association* 88 (2015): 145–53.

natural friendship, according to which each one, inasmuch as he is, seeks and desires his end God as first cause and supreme being.[24]

Natural principles effect a friendly union with God. However, full friendship inclusive of the key marks of interpersonal union, especially mutual indwelling, requires the supernatural grace in the form of charity, to which we will turn in the next section.

In terms of natural principles alone, the natural love of God can go astray in a variety of ways through vices opposed to religion, such as superstition and idolatry. Through these vices, a person fails to unite himself properly to God. This is not bad for God insofar as human vices cannot harm him. However, it is bad for the human being and leads to the undermining of well-being. By failing to love God properly, a person's self-love becomes structurally disordered. One reason for this is fairly simple. Part of what makes self-love proper is the willing of appropriate goods to oneself. If human beings are ordained to God as their end, an end realized at the natural level by uniting oneself to him in loving reverence, then the vices opposed to religion necessarily undermine proper self-love.

The deeper reason that the failure to love God harms the love of self concerns the same metaphysical ground for love in general. Substantial unity for every creature, but in particular human beings, is a derivative reality. Just as union derives from unity, so (created) unity derives from God through participation. At the level of love, just as the love of neighbor receives its nature and characteristics from the love of self, so an analogous point is true for the love of self in relation to the love of God. To be fully proper, the love of self must connect to God in keeping with the structure of participation, which entails that the love of God must exceed the love of self. Thus, the vices opposed to religion involve acting contrary to the metaphysical foundation of the love of God and love of self.

The more ensconced the vices become, the more disordered self-love becomes. Moreover, as the previous chapters have covered,

---

24. Aquinas, *Commentary on the First Letter of Saint Paul to the Corinthians*, 806.

proper self-love is a necessary condition to the loving union with others. Thus, the vices opposed to religion—the failures to love God properly—undercut both self-love and the love of others. The vices lead to the disintegration introduced in chapter 1. The virtue of religion, by contrast, properly aligns one to God, which cultivates proper self-love. Thereby, by extension, it promotes loving unions with others.

To make his case, we again find Aquinas drawing upon a principle of Dionysius that "everything loves itself with a love that holds it together." A person's appetites, both sensitive and rational, adapt or conform to the object to which they unite.

> Consequently love of a suitable good perfects and betters the lover; but love of a good which is unsuitable to the lover, wounds and worsens him. Wherefore man is perfected and bettered chiefly by the love of God: but is wounded and worsened by the love of sin.[25]

The next two chapters will explore more fully the deformation and perfection of love, and the previous discussion provides the key principle to both. Since the person conforms himself to that which he loves, he is perfected only by appropriate goods. Due to his metaphysical connection to God, this means that his self-love can only be proper if first directed to the whole, perfect good/God. Sin draws one away from God and therefore inevitably wounds and worsens first the love of self, and then the love of others.

In short, the metaphysical relations underlying and determining the directions and parameters of the love constitute both the union of similitude with other human beings and, by participation, the appropriate basis for the love of God over oneself. The unity of an individual human person provides the proximate center of gravity for union with other human persons. A person seeks an affective and real union with others that approximates his own unity. The more the union between lover and beloved approximates unity, the closer and more intense the relationship between them. Due to the reliance

---

25. *ST* I-II, q. 28, a. 5.

of each individual on God's existence and goodness, God forms the ultimate center of gravity in the life of the person. Participation in God constitutes the metaphysical root and foundation for a person's substantial unity. Thereby, just as the quality of one's love of others depends upon the quality of his prior love of self, so the quality of his love of self depends upon the quality of his love of God.

Aquinas bases all of this on natural principles. God loves human beings with a love of friendship, but a mutual friendship with God is not naturally possible. While human beings have a natural similitude with God in virtue of being created in his image and likeness, the relation is asymmetrical: God does not have a similitude with human beings. Thus, a true, mutual friendship union with God cannot occur. However, at the supernatural level, Aquinas holds that friendship with God can and does occur through the virtue of charity. Let us turn to the nature of this friendship.

THE SUPERNATURAL LOVE OF GOD

Due to God's infinite superiority, human beings cannot have a natural similitude and, therefore, a natural friendship with him. Yet, Aquinas characterizes charity as friendship with God. Thus, friendship is possible, but only supernaturally. For such a friendship to occur, God must overcome the lack of similitude, the lack of sufficient equality, found in the natural relationship between him and human beings to establish a mutual union of friendship. Aquinas employs the notion of communication (*communicatio*) to explain how God establishes a sufficient equality to allow for a true friendship in a literal sense of the term. In the passage from the *Commentary on I Corinthians* cited in the previous section, Aquinas remarks that there is a communication from God solely in terms of natural goods. This allows for worship and effects a natural union with God. Through grace, a greater communication occurs, which makes possible an even greater union.

Participation and the Love of God

Accordingly, since there is a communication between man and God, inasmuch as He communicates His happiness to us, some kind of friendship must needs be based on the same communication.... The love which is based on this communication, is charity: wherefore it is evident that charity is the friendship of man for God.[26]

Elaborating on the nature and role of communication, Joseph Bobik notes:

Whenever two persons, a superior and an inferior, have nothing in common, but the superior offers a shareable gift to the inferior, not only do the two begin thereby to have something in common ... which makes friendship between them *possible*, but *it becomes fitting* that the inferior respond to the initiative of the superior by doing whatever he can *to help make actual* the friendship to which he has been invited.[27]

God offers a share in his life through the indwelling of the Holy Spirit. It thereby becomes fitting for the human being to reciprocate by cultivating the relationship.

As discussed in chapter 2, the union of similitude admits of degrees. Similitude derives from a comparison to a person's own unity or identity. By nature, some people approximate one's own unity more closely than others. By choice, particularly through the indissoluble marriage oath, persons can mutually quasi-extend their unity to one another. On account of the gulf necessitated by God's superiority over human beings, a person cannot establish such a friendship by choice with God. God, however, can choose to extend himself to the human person. God's communication of his life and happiness represent his choice to extend himself in the way necessary to establish the conditions for friendship. As a choice, divine communication constitutes a gratuitous act transcending natural principles and the requirements of nature.

Given the gratuity inherent in God's communication, the act is supernatural. To this point, the focus of this text has been principal-

---

26. *ST* II-II, q. 23, a. 1.
27. Joseph Bobik, "Aquinas on *Communicatio*: The Foundation of Friendship and Caritas," *Modern Schoolman* 64 (1986): 15.

ly upon Aquinas's philosophical understanding of unity, union, and love. I have ventured into his theology mostly to clarify what he considers natural versus supernatural principles. This section transitions to his full account as inclusive of both natural and supernatural principles. This full account is worth understanding for three reasons. First, it is Aquinas's complete account. If we wish to do interpretive justice to his thought, we need to incorporate both dimensions. Second, the supernatural principles affirmed by Aquinas in his theological account of charity build upon natural principles. Since he contends that grace perfects nature, Aquinas's understanding of love as perfected by charity offers us fuller insight into what he contends is the full realization of the natural reality. This point is similar to the methodological approach stated in chapter 1; Aquinas uses the perfect instance of a thing to best understand its nature. Charity is the greatest cultivation of the will and most perfect form of love, in his view. Third, if one accepts Aquinas's theological principles, then understanding charity is not merely a means of better understanding natural love, but a potential source of insight into the true ultimate nature of love itself.

The previous sections treated a person's participation in the universal good/God as the cause of an inner pull toward goodness within each person's conscious experience. In effect, the metaphysical connection of participation serves as the efficient cause of the human inclination to love God. Charity treats God as the final cause of a love. Healing the wounds of original sin, charity removes the obstacles to the possibility of loving God more than self by properly aligning a person to God and bringing about an affective and real union with him.

Aversion from God, which is brought about by sin, is removed by charity, but not by knowledge alone: hence charity, by the love of God, unites the soul immediately to Him with a chain of spiritual union.[28]

---

28. *ST* II-II, q. 27, a. 4, ad 3.

For Aquinas, charity is principally friendship with God, inclusive of the characteristics of love and friendship previously discussed—melting, ecstasy, mutual indwelling, communication/sharing, trust, longing, benevolence, beneficence, delight, and concord.

Charity, particularly perfect charity, involves a maximal mode of all these properties. Aquinas appeals to both natural and supernatural reasons to account for the higher mode of these properties within divine friendship. We have already seen in the case of human friendships how the intensity of the friendship increases in proportion to the union's approximation to unity. As the two hearts approach oneness, the intimacy and depth of the union become more pronounced. We looked at the progression of intensity, if you will, among ordinary friends, kin, children, and finally spouses.

If marriage provides the potential for the greatest human union by way of the closest approximation to unity, each human being's participation in God establishes the potential for something greater. The human person's metaphysical connection to God, whereby his unity necessarily relates to him by participation, is something more fundamental than considerations of unity taken on its own. In a literal sense, for Aquinas, a person is closer to God than he is to himself, or, stated differently, a person's identity is inherently related to God as the source of his being and goodness. The relation of each human being to God in virtue of participation creates the natural foundation for a permanent and intense relationship with God. Such a friendship remains only a potentiality unless God establishes a sufficient equality for it. Once God makes possible a friendship with a human being by condescending to him, a person can become actually united to him in the most intense loving union possible for a human being (the union of divine persons to one another represents the most intense loving union *simpliciter*).

Turning to the properties of divine friendship, we see that many of them find their source in natural principles and are then elevated by grace. Divine benevolence and beneficence take the form of providence. Divine providence involves all the goods requisite for human flourishing, including material goods. However, providence over human beings, as rational creatures, goes well beyond the providing of material necessities. Aquinas speaks here of the natural moral law.

> Wherefore, since all things subject to Divine providence are ruled and measured by the eternal law, as was stated above; it is evident that all things partake somewhat of the eternal law, in so far as, namely, from its being imprinted on them, they derive their respective inclinations to their proper acts and ends. Now among all others, the rational creature is subject to Divine providence in the most excellent way, in so far as it partakes of a share of providence, by being provident both for itself and for others. Wherefore it has a share of the Eternal Reason, whereby it has a natural inclination to its proper act and end: and this participation of the eternal law in the rational creature is called the natural law.... It is therefore evident that the natural law is nothing else than the rational creature's participation in the eternal law.[29]

God provides for human beings by benevolently willing the good to them and bestowing the goods through beneficence.

Importantly, for Aquinas, providence over human beings includes the good of self-governance. God bestows goods on human beings, goods that they have more or less passively received—for instance, existence. However, God also provides human beings with the abilities to provide for themselves. *Prudentia* or prudence, the virtue of practical reasons, most basically is a person's providence over his own life. Aquinas identifies foresight or providence as the key integral part of prudence.

> Whenever many things are requisite for a unity, one of them must needs be the principal to which all the other are subordinate. Hence in every whole one part must be formal and predominate, whence the whole has a unity. Accordingly foresight is the principal of all the parts of prudence.[30]

Practically speaking, this means that the good of human nature necessarily includes activity in the form of a conscious pursuit of the good. The human good includes the loving friendships with others,

29. *ST* I-II, q. 91, a. 2.
30. *ST* II-II, q. 49, a. 6.

and part of the way God provides for human beings is through the protecting and sustaining of the capacities necessary for friendship. Such providence takes on a special significance in the context of charity insofar as divine providence becomes constitutive of friendship with God himself. God provides for human beings in such a manner as to draw them into a union with himself.

By emphasizing the individual directedness of divine providence over human beings, Aquinas places the foundation of divine friendship at the natural level.

> Furthermore, the [individual] rational creature is subject to divine providence in such a way that he is not only governed thereby, but is also able to know the rational plan of providence in some way. Hence, it is appropriate for him to exercise providence and government over other things. This is not the case with other creatures, for they participate in providence only to the extent of being subordinate to it. Through this possession of the capacity to exercise providence one may also direct and govern his own acts. So, the rational creature participates in divine providence, not only by being governed passively, but also by governing actively, for he governs himself in his personal acts.[31]

God exercises providence over nonrational beings according to the species and not so much for the individual *qua* individual. Rational beings are different. Insofar as each person is incommunicable and distinct from even other human beings, God attends to each as an individual. Friendship is a sort of natural progression from this. A human being cannot literally be friends with humanity. Rather, he can only be friends with individuals. One unity must encounter another unity—one heart of two. God's benevolence and beneficence raised to the level of friendship must be personalized or directed to the individual *qua* individual.

From the human side of friendship with God, benevolence and beneficence principally concern three things: the proper love of self, proper self-governance, and the proper love of neighbor. The order of charity is God, self, and neighbor. Charity unites a human being

31. *ScG* III, c. 113, p. 5.

to God in the loving union of friendship. Out of the love of God, though, a person should love himself and all other human beings in light of their relation to God. A human being cannot will and acquire goods for God directly, and thus benevolence and beneficence do not directly relate to God as object. However, because of the love of God, a person should will and acquire the good for himself and for others.

As charity perfects nature, the natural order of love of self over others remains in charity. Again, the basic principle Aquinas employs is "just as unity surpasses union, the fact that a man himself has a share of the Divine good, is a more potent reason for loving than that another should be a partner with him in that share."[32] Through charity, a person has both a more intense love of self—an increased fervor to will and acquire goods for oneself—and a greater good to will and seek. The greater good in question is the real union with God. Since the love of self serves as the natural model and impulse for love of others, the more a person wills the divine good to himself, the more he shall will it to the others, as well. Thus, the charitable love of self promotes the charitable love of neighbor.

In terms of the connection between proper self-governance and charity, Thomistic self-governance at its core is the willing, pursuit, and acquisition of goods for oneself. Self-governance, due to benevolence and beneficence forming two of self-love's essential properties, derives from self-love. Consequently, charity directly perfects the activity of self-governance. The reason for this is that charity "directs the acts of all other virtues to the last end."[33] Based on human nature, self-governance derives from self-love, and the better a person loves himself, the more effectively he governs himself. Charity perfects self-love and thus, by extension, self-governance, as well. The next two chapters will cover the specifics of charitable self-governance, both in terms of its absence and full actuality.

Continuing with the marks of divine friendship from God's per-

32. *ST* II-II, q. 26, a. 4.
33. *ST* II-II, q. 23, a. 8.

spective first, I will group together the characteristics of melting, longing, ecstasy, mutual indwelling, and conversation. A lover longs both for the continued existence of and a union with the beloved—particularly a real, fully affective, and conscious union. Insofar as God loves human beings necessarily with a love of friendship versus a love of concupiscence—willing the good to each human being for his own sake—God longs for the human response. This should be interpreted analogically as compatible with God's unchanging perfection, but the gist of the position is that the very nature of divine love is a call or invitation to union with God. Since God himself is the good willed in divine love, God's act of willing the good to each human being represents the act of willing himself to each human being. At the natural level, as we saw, the union with God principally comes through the virtue of religion—uniting oneself to God in worship and reverence. God gives to the human being the abilities to unite with him in this way. At the supernatural level, the invitation is to the loving union of friendship to the full depths of mutual indwelling (by the action of the Holy Spirit), sharing, and conversing.

Aquinas cites the gifts of the Holy Spirit as one of key ways by which God shares his life with the beloved in friendship.[34] This includes the traditional sevenfold gifts of wisdom, knowledge, understanding, counsel, fortitude, piety, and fear of the Lord, but Aquinas expands the meaning of gifts to encompass all of the infused virtues. "Man needs yet higher perfections, whereby to be disposed to be moved by God. These perfections are called gifts ... because by them man is disposed to become amenable to Divine inspiration."[35] The gifts are a direct infusion and sharing of God's life into the life of the person. The effect of these gifts relates to a deepening of the loving indwelling between God and the person.

In terms of God's conversing with human beings, Aquinas identifies contemplation as the key way by which this occurs.

---

34. *ScG* IV, c. 21, p. 7
35. *ST* I-II, q. 68, a. 1.

The conversation of man to God is by contemplation of Him.... Since, therefore, the Holy Spirit makes us lovers of God, we are in consequence established by the Holy Spirit as contemplators of God. Hence, the Apostle says: "But we all beholding the glory of the Lord with open face, are transformed into the same image from glory to glory, as by the Spirit of the Lord." (2 Cor 3:18)[36]

Aquinas begins with the perspective of the human person to God. The human lover converses with the divine beloved by prayerfully contemplating him. God as lover elevates the nature of this conversation to allow the beloved—the human lover—to become more and more like God himself. God reveals and conveys his heart to the beloved by allowing the beloved to become more like him.

To address these properties of divine friendship from the perspective of the human being, let us begin with longing and ecstasy. Human beings need not be closed off and isolated within themselves. While this fact has an obvious application to the context of interpersonal human relationships, it also applies here. The natural orientation of self-love extends outward. As we saw in the previous section, a human person experiences a pull toward goods, and the greater the good, the greater the pull. God as the whole good inclines a properly self-loving person to go out of himself and adapt or conform to that good. Divine friendship provides the ultimate satisfaction to that longing. The mutual indwelling in terms of divinely elevated contemplation then works to perfect the person himself, which in turns serves to increase a proper love of self. Aquinas offers straightforward reasoning for this point: through self-love, a person loves his own goodness, and his own goodness increases in the measure that he becomes transformed to God. Thus, there is more to love, so to speak, in his love of self.

Regarding the notion of melting, in divine friendship, it only applies to the human side of the relationship. God has no hardness of heart. For reasons we will discuss more fully in chapter 5, human beings do not always desire their true good even when clearly appre-

---

36. *ScG* IV, c. 22, p. 2.

hending such good. Loving the good involves adapting or conforming oneself to that good. Pride and disordered self-love act against the acquiescence central to adaptation. Resistance to love proves to be a threat to any friendship, human or divine. In the perfect union of divine friendship in heaven, resistance will not occur. In this life, it does. Therefore, divine friendship requires melting on the part of the human person—a readiness and willingness to allow the ecstasy and mutual indwelling of love to occur.

In terms of delight, Aquinas focuses on the human side of friendship with God. The key affective characteristic of friendship is the delight friends take in the presence of the other (and negatively, the sorrow caused by the absence of the other). As this delight is mutual, it forms a true union of affections between friends. The satisfaction of any appetite causes delight, and the satisfaction of the rational appetite or will specifically causes joy. Friendship produces both the delight of the sense appetites and the will. Joy is the chief form of delight in both human and divine friendship, but particularly in the latter. Charity effects joy in the lover by the possession or union with God. As the union with God in this life pales in comparison to the union in the next life, the joy a person experiences now is only incomplete and partial. However, the hope of a full union in the life to come occasions an additional joy of expectation. Moreover, in times of suffering, the joy of charity proves to be a source of great consolation. Such consolation, while providing solace in its own right, serves to remind the lover of the perfect joy yet to be had and thus spurs him on to greater hope.

The final property of friendship we will consider is concord, or the unity of wills. Between human friends, concord results from the mutual core beliefs and willing of the same sorts of goods. In the case of a true human friendship, each friend properly loves himself and thereby wills the appropriate goods to himself. In friendship, each friend extends such willing of appropriate goods outward to the other, which effects a union of wills or concord between them. The concord found in divine friendship takes on a different character. Even though God creates a quasi-equality between him and human beings to make friendship possible, he remains superior to human beings. This asymmetry has an impact on all the properties of friendship to some degree. In the case of concord, the chief difference concerns strict conformity. In human friendships, concord involves mutual consent and not a strict conformity out of obedience to the will of the other. In divine friendship, such obedience is necessary. The next chapter will lay the groundwork for the appropriateness of conforming to the divine will, and chapter 5 will address conformity and obedience directly. Let us turn, then, to these analyses.

4

Conformity and Sin

THE NECESSITY OF CONFORMITY

Due to the relationship between unity and union, the ways in which a person relates to oneself in self-love forms the basis for relating to others. Due to the relationship between participation in God and unity, the ways in which a person relates to God determines the quality of the love of self. A proper love of God promotes a sustainable proper love of self. Therefore, a proper love of God promotes a proper love of others. We have discussed that this is the case for Aquinas, but we have not fully examined why it is the case. The next two chapters treat the latter question more thoroughly.

For Aquinas, appetites are passive powers. What moves the appetites to act is that which attracts them in some way.[1] That which attracts them is the good, either as perceived through the senses or as apprehended by the intellect. We have discussed this under the aspect of the union of similitude. When a person perceives a likeness or favorability with another person, his will is naturally drawn to enter into union with the other. The appetites, both the sense and rational, seek a union with the good. Due to the unions of affection and possession, the process involves the affective dimensions

---

1. See *ST* I-II, q. 26, a. 1.

of complacency for the good and delight in the obtainment of the good. We have seen Aquinas appeal to Dionysius's principle that love is a uniting and binding force. Through love, a person becomes bound with the good sought.

The terms "union of possession" and "real union" perhaps do not immediately convey the full significance of what occurs through love. A person does not possess some good as an object distinct from himself. Rather, to possess the good, he must adapt and conform himself to it in a fundamental manner. His will is shaped by what he loves. Aquinas's response to whether love wounds the lover nicely summarizes a good deal of this aspect of his philosophy of love.

> Love denotes a certain adapting of the appetitive power to some good. Now nothing is hurt by being adapted to that which is suitable to it; rather, if possible, it is perfected and bettered. But if a thing be adapted to that which is not suitable to it, it is hurt and made worse thereby. Consequently love of a suitable good perfects and betters the lover; but love of a good which is unsuitable to the lover, wounds and worsens him. Wherefore man is perfected and bettered chiefly by the love of God: but is wounded and worsened by the love of sin.[2]

A colloquialism tells us that a person is what he eats. Aquinas affirms something even more fundamental—namely, a person, to a significant degree, is what he loves. By loving anything, a person conforms himself to that thing. Due to the fact that every action springs from love,[3] through every act performed, a person adapts and conforms himself to the end willed.

Through a sense appetite or will, conformity is the adaption of oneself to the object loved, particularly in terms of a real union with it. Accordingly, conformity forms part of the very structure of action itself. One cannot act without conforming to the end sought. For Aquinas, then, conformity of its nature is neither good nor bad. It receives its specification from the end. If a person pursues and obtains

---

2. *ST* I-II, q. 28, a. 5.
3. "Every agent acts for an end.... Now the end is the good desired and loved by each one. Wherefore it is evident that every agent, whatever it be, does every action from love of some kind"; *ST* I-II, q. 28, a. 6.

Conformity and Sin

a suitable good, the adaption in question benefits him. The pursuit and acquisition of an unsuitable good, on the other hand, harm and wound him. In short, the active life cannot be about avoiding conformity. Rather, those things to which a person conforms himself generates the most dramatic elements of the ethical life. This sort of conformity essential to the nature of action itself forms the foundational layer within Aquinas's understanding of self-determination. Through love and the various actions it prompts, a person shapes himself by conforming and adapting to the goods or perceived goods sought. A person "approaches non-existence" by conforming to the wrong sorts of things, while conformity to the good contributes to greater being, unity, and personal integration.[4]

Due to substantial unity, a person must love himself by seeking and acquiring goods for himself. The natural orientation of the love of self toward the good disposes a person to adapt himself to that which betters him. Moreover, the natural love of God perfects the love of self, which facilitates both a joyful interior life and the proper love of others. This raises the question of why people often choose the wrong sorts of things. Aquinas contends that the most fundamental answer to this question is disordered self-love, which in turn begets all sorts of other sins.

In chapter 1, I gave the basic argument as to why Aquinas holds disordered love to be the cause of every sin: all actions, both good and sinful, proceed from the will. The basic act of the will is love, in particular the love of self, and all actions spring from this love. Since sinful actions are indeed actions, love, particularly in the form of the love of self, must motivate them, as well. However, by definition, proper self-love cannot cause sin. Thus, the cause of sin must be improper self-love, for which Aquinas also uses the terms "disordered," "inordinate," and "wicked" love of self.

The proper and direct cause of sin is to be considered on the part of the adherence to a mutable good; in which respect every sinful act proceeds from inordinate desire for some temporal good. Now the fact that anyone

---

4. Aquinas, *On Truth*, q. 23, a. 7.

desires a temporal good inordinately, is due to the fact that he loves himself inordinately.... Therefore it is evident that inordinate love of self is the cause of every sin.[5]

Given that disordered self-love causes all other sinful acts, Aquinas must account for how the love of self itself becomes disordered. He identifies pride as the chief culprit, but pride is not a notion altogether distinct from disordered self-love. Rather, it is a way of talking about how the love of self becomes disordered.

Pride is the inordinate desire for one's own excellence.[6] In an act of sin, there is a conversion or turning toward an apparent good and an aversion from an appropriate good. The ultimate good from which the prideful person turns away is God—particularly the proper act of uniting to him naturally in religion and supernaturally in charity. Aquinas considers whether pride or inordinate self-love is the cause of sin. He responds with the following:

> In desiring to excel, man loves himself, for to love oneself is the same as to desire some good for oneself. Consequently, it amounts to the same whether we reckon pride or self-love as the beginning of every evil.[7]

Through a prideful self-love, a person turns away from union with God and, by extension, full union with others, for the sake of dwelling excessively with oneself. According to Aquinas, in the case of the devil's fall, Satan preferred himself to union with God and did so entirely in the absence of temptation or immoderate inclinations. Likewise, in the case of Adam and Eve, the same basic act occurred, though preceded by demonic temptation.

Fallen human nature, as an effect of original sin, has disordered passions, such that there is a pull toward immoderate goods. However, the same root of sin remains: prideful self-love. A person chooses to love only his own unity—his own self as isolated from anything else—above all else. To put it more strongly, through disordered

---

5. *ST* I-II, q. 77, a. 4.
6. *ST* II-II, q. 162, a. 1, ad 2.
7. *ST* I-II, q. 84, a. 2, ad 2.

self-love, he eschews what is his true relational identity in favor of an artificially constructed nonrelational identity. As discussed in chapter 3, each human being's unity and identity necessarily relate to God through participation in him. Consequently, the prideful person relates to a version of himself that is illusory. By its nature, the choice to love oneself excessively turns oneself inward toward immanence and away from ecstasy and transcendence. To do this, he must resist the proper cultivation of his self-love found in the love of God, a resistance that ultimately undermines his ability to enter into union with other human beings.

Human beings must conform to something. If they do not actively choose to love God above self, they will necessarily conform the good of their selves as the highest good. To do so is unsuitable, as the human being is not the highest good, even for oneself. Pride, as the most basic failure to love appropriately, leads to other sins. All such sins represent distinct ways of failing to love appropriately. From the metaphysical perspective, sinful ways of acting are simply ways of acting contrary to the orientation of unity deriving from participation in God and union flowing from unity. Due to sin's trajectory away from what is ultimately real, the effects of sin cannot help but be destructive, especially to the sinner himself. To assess the exact nature of this self-destruction, or undermining of one's own unity, let us turn to Aquinas's understanding of sin and hatred and its necessary connections to unity, union, and love.

SIN AND HATRED

Sin, broadly characterized, consists of any inordinate act that fundamentally involves an aversion from or failure to conform to God. Objectively, sin refers to the ways in which an action, both by way of commission and omission, undermines a person's substantial unity and the associated proper love of self. Subjectively, sin involves such acts being done with some form of morally deficient intent. As human love follows the structure of participation, unity, and union, it has the three forms of the love of God, the love of self, and the love of others. Consequently, a person can fail to appropriately love God, self, and others; thus, we have a threefold division of sin.

Aquinas contends that this threefold order of love involves three kinds of laws specifying three kinds of goods to which a person can fail to conform: divine law, natural moral law, and the civil law. Mirroring the metaphysical order or participation, unity, and union upon which it rests, the rule of proper love follows the same order.

> For whatever things are comprised under the order of reason, are comprised under the order of God Himself.... In like manner, [the order of reason] includes [the civil order] and surpasses it, because in all things we are directed according to the order of reason.[8]

Proper laws are nothing other than what directs human beings to the good. They indicate those things to which love should be directed and those things to which love should not be directed. For Aquinas, the three orders of law pertain to the three orders of love. Thereby, the rules of reason and civil law are contained under divine law.

Sin, as a perversion of love, acts against the good in these three areas. A person can sin directly against God, self, or neighbor, but sins in the latter two categories make necessary reference to those that precede it. Proper self-love forms the basis for the love of neighbor. Sins against one's neighbor, while corruptive of the love of neighbor, include a sin against oneself. Put another way, a person acting entirely on proper self-love cannot sin against his neighbor. There is first a disorder in his self-love that then manifests itself relationally against another person. Similarly, proper self-love depends upon the love of God. A person cannot sin against himself without sinning against God. Thus, all sin, not just acts explicitly contrary to God, involves a failure to love God appropriately. The seven deadly or capital sins and the ultimate sources from which they flow capture and reflect this threefold ordering in Aquinas's thought.

The traditional list of seven deadly sins includes pride, envy,

---

8. *ST* I-II, q. 72, a. 4.

wrath, sloth, greed, gluttony, and lust. Moreover, this ordering is not accidental. The order is meant to capture pride as the gravest of all sins and the decreasing severity of disorder from pride as the most to lust as the least disordered. This list comes from early Christian to medieval reflections and discussions on the predominant causes of sin. We find these exact seven sins identified by Dante in the *Purgatorio*. However, Aquinas offers a slightly different list. For his part, instead of characterizing pride as the worst deadly sin, he treats covetousness and pride more gravely as the roots of all sin and not as the more specific deadly sins.⁹ He does so for the reasons discussed in the previous section. Pride and wicked self-love are nuances of the same act (and over time form a habit). To desire one's own excellence as the highest good is to desire goods inordinately for oneself and to turn away from God, who is seen as a threat to one's status as the highest good. In place of pride on his list, Aquinas follows St. Gregory the Great in treating vainglory, a distinct species of pride, as the first, with the remaining six equating to Dante's—and now traditional—list.

As another point of comparison with the now traditional list, it might seem peculiar that Aquinas treats covetousness or avarice twice: first as a general root of all sin and as second as a specific sin. In both *De Malo* and the *Summa Theologiae*, he clarifies that we can characterize covetousness in a broad sense concerning the inordinate desire for any good or in the more specific sense concerning an inordinate desire for money and riches.

Avarice as to the primary application of the name signifies the inordinate desire for money.... And so inasmuch as money is a special matter, it seems that avarice as to the primary application of the name is a special kind of sin. But we by an analogy amplify the name *avarice* to signify inordinate desire for any good, and avarice in this sense is sin in general, since every sin involves a turning toward a transitory good through inordinate desire.¹⁰

9. *ST* I-II, q. 84.
10. Aquinas, *On Evil*, trans. Richard Regan (Oxford: Oxford University Press, 2003), q. XIII, a. 1; compare *ST* I-II, q. 84, a. 1. This work dates to the second half of the 1260s; see Torrell, *Saint Thomas Aquinas*, 201–7.

Covetousness in the broad sense, then, is another name for inordinate self-love.

According to Aquinas, the first four sins on the list are properly spiritual, and the last three are carnal as pertaining to bodily appetites. Sins take their severity from what they oppose. Spiritual sins directly involve turning away from God and toward oneself, whereas carnal sins directly pertain more to the turning toward bodily goods and only indirectly to turning away from God. In addition, the harm caused to one's neighbor due to the turning away from God tends to far exceed the relational harm caused to neighbor due to carnal sins.[11] Aquinas contends that the sins against one's own body are less severe than sins against one's neighbor. Thus, the immoderate desires for money, food, drink, and sex, while perennial sources of sin, constitute a milder disorder of love versus the spiritual sins. Spiritual sins are, thereby, graver by nature, though in practice a person might struggle more with the carnal sins. In those instances, the carnal sins represent a more pressing threat, but remain essentially less severe. Nonetheless, the carnal sins have the same ultimate root as the spiritual sins—prideful, wicked self-love. Moreover, spiritual sin, while essentially worse than the carnal variety, tends to give rise to the carnal sins. Let us turn to each of the seven deadly sins and how they specifically draw a person away from the natural orientation toward goodness as rooted in participation, unity, and union.

Vainglory is essentially a relational form of pride. Through vainglory, the prideful person seeks honor and glory from others commensurate with what he perceives to be the level of his excellence. Envy is sorrow over another person's good. In appropriate love, a person should desire and seek the good to his neighbor. Through pride, one's self-love is disordered and seeks the good in an inherently self-serving manner. Prideful self-love cannot extend to others

---

11. I make the case in Anthony T. Flood, "The Destructiveness of Lust and Its Cure: Reflections on Dante, Aquinas, and Wojtyla" (in *Woman as Prophet in the Home and the World*, ed. R. Mary Hayden Lemmons [Lanham, Md.: Lexington, 2016], 163–76), that Aquinas fails to account adequately for the relational harm—the harm done to others—caused by lust.

with a love of friendship. The good of another becomes a threat to one's self-estimation. Instead of self-love naturally extending to the love of another, pride begets envy that not only withholds love from another, but cannot even tolerate the good of others.

Vainglory and envy, thereby, produce a double detrimental effect. First, such a person experiences a naturally good thing—the good of one's neighbor—as bad. Second, the person does not will good to the neighbor. These effects of sin begin the process whereby self-preoccupation culminates in self-isolation. We will return to this effecting of self-isolation after treating the remaining sins, but at this point, it should be obvious that by resisting the natural inclination of unity toward union—self-love to the love of others—the end result will inevitably be an isolated mode of being.

Envy begets anger or wrath. Anger chiefly concerns the proper response to some perceived wrong done to a person and, as rooted in the irascible appetite, is natural and good in itself. In this respect, anger shares a similarity with the pleasures connected to the concupiscible appetite, which also possesses a natural goodness. In this sense, both anger and pleasure have a proper place in a well-ordered life. However, anger can become immoderate in two (nonmutually exclusive) ways and, as immoderate, represents a deadly sin.

Too much anger clouds reason and undermines clear choice. Such immoderate anger may well be in reaction to a legitimate wrong, but once anger undermines reason it becomes problematic. More importantly, sinful anger tends to result from envy, thus the estimation of the threat posed by the neighbor is illusory. Prideful self-love disposes a person to lash out at his neighbor. His bloated sense of self first causes envy at a neighbor's good and then anger at the neighbor himself. This dynamic creates a vicious circle: the more the anger clouds his judgment, the more he misestimates his neighbor, and, consequently, the more anger he experiences. The greater one's pride—the greater one's disordered love of self—the more of a "threat" the neighbor poses. Thus, the greater one's pride, the greater the anger directed toward one's neighbor.

Finally, in terms of the spiritual sins, Aquinas lists sloth, defining it as a "sorrow for spiritual good."[12] He also quotes Damascene's even stronger gloss of sloth as "*an oppressive sorrow*," to which Aquinas adds that it "so weighs upon man's mind, that he wants to do nothing."[13] Sloth might seem strange as a spiritual sin, particularly if one understands it to be reducible to laziness. It is true that sloth would undercut a person's motivation to seek the good of his neighbor, but compared to the sins just listed, sloth seems mild. I have found Rebecca Konyndyk DeYoung's work on Aquinas's account of sloth particularly instructive in showing just how destructive Aquinas considers sloth to be.[14] She draws attention to how Aquinas opposes sloth explicitly to the virtue of charity. Most fundamentally, sloth is not plain laziness, but a resistance or aversion to the love of God, which can manifest itself in either inertia or restlessness.

Etymologically and literally, *acedia* means "absence—or lack—of care." The desert fathers viewed the slothful absence of care as particularly troubling for a monk. They diagnose it as one of the great impediments to monastic life, since it threatens the core identity of the monk himself. DeYoung states:

> Like Evagrius, Cassian thinks sloth is a serious spiritual vice because it threatens one's fundamental identity as one who has devoted one's life to developing a relationship with God and erodes one's commitment to the religious community formed by that identity.[15]

A monk plagued by sloth shrinks from his identity as related to God. Sloth manifests itself as idleness and inactivity insofar as the monk fails to pray or engage in spiritual exercises and activity. Just

---

12. *ST* II-II, q. 35, a. 2.
13. *ST* II-II, q. 35, a. 1.
14. Rebecca Konyndyk DeYoung has several works on the subject of Aquinas's account of sloth: "Resistance to the Demands of Love: Aquinas on the Vice of *Acedia*," *Thomist* 68, no. 2 (2004): 173–204; "Aquinas on the Vice of Sloth: Three Interpretive Issues," *Thomist* 75, no. 1 (2011): 43–64; and "Sloth: Some Historical Reflections on Laziness, Effort, and the Resistance to the Demands of Love," in *Virtues and Their Vices*, ed. Kevin Timpe and Craig A. Boyd (Oxford: Oxford University Press, 2014), 177–98.
15. DeYoung, "Sloth: Some Historical Reflections," 181.

as often, though, sloth manifests itself as restlessness and business insofar as the monk engages in various activities as a means of distraction from prayer and spiritual exercises.

Building upon this view of the desert fathers, Aquinas broadens both the intension and extension of sloth by identifying it not merely as a monastic vice, but as a vice relevant to the Christian life itself. Sloth is a mortal sin not just for those in the religious life, but for any Christian. The reason is that sloth stands in direct opposition to charity, particularly in terms of the divine indwelling within the person made possible through charity.

> Mortal sin is so called because it destroys the spiritual life which is the effect of charity, whereby God dwells in us. Wherefore any sin which by its very nature is contrary to charity is a mortal sin by reason of its genus. And such is sloth, because the proper effect of charity is joy in God ... while sloth is sorrow about spiritual good in as much as it is a Divine good.[16]

The sorrow concerning the divine good derives directly from the will itself—a person's willed resistance to the divine good within him.[17]

Analogous to how the desert fathers perceive sloth as a threat to the very identity of the monk, Aquinas understands sloth to attack a person's identity as a person in a conscious, love-based relation to God. Again, DeYoung states:

> Sloth's main target is our love relationship with God, in the context of a life in which we take our likeness to God to be our defining identity and loving communion with God to be our main vocation as human beings. The slothful person resists this relationship and the like-naturedness to God that she must accept and cultivate to sustain it.[18]

The slothful person may very well be lazy and averse to doing much. However, he also might be a busybody or restless, doing just about anything as a distraction or diversion from accepting the demands

---

16. *ST* II-II, q. 35, a. 3.
17. DeYoung, "Sloth: Some Historical Reflections," 188.
18. Ibid., 189.

of being in relation to God. As Aquinas succinctly puts it, "Spiritual apathy indeed immobilizes the persons subject to it from the things that cause their sadness but renders them prone to contrary things."[19]

Sloth, like vainglory, envy, and anger, is primarily an aversion to a noncarnal good and the love a person should have for such a good. In all four cases, a person retreats within himself and isolates himself from the proper union with God and communion with others. Given the ways in which participation, unity, and union interrelate, a person's identity is not self-contained, but rather relational. In addition, the relationality is twofold: relational as fundamentally related to God through participation and secondarily as related to others, as unity gravitates toward union. Through disordered self-love, a person attempts to impose on his true nature a nonrelational identity. By cutting himself off from God through pride, his disordered self-love is not capable of genuinely willing the good to others. As the severity of disordered self-love increases, he cannot even experience another person as a good. Other persons are competitors—threats of which to be wary and about which to be angry.

In the place of the good of union with others, the wicked person gravitates toward bodily goods—wealth and the pleasures of food, drink, and sex. As these goods are sought without due consideration for others or for one's true good, the desires rapidly become immoderate: greed, the immoderate desire for wealth; gluttony, the immoderate desire for food and drink; lust, the immoderate desire for sex. All these factors reinforce the artificially created nonrelational identity, and all of them combine to effect a voluntary self-isolation, or "willed loneliness," as Stump terms it. However, though such an identity is contrary to the metaphysical order, over the long term, the sinful person will become either spiteful, slothfully listless, or both. In whichever case, a person lives contrary to the union with God and union with neighbor to which his natural orientations point.

---

19. Aquinas, *On Evil*, q. XI, a. 4, ad 2.

Living one's life in a manner contrary to the appropriate order of God, self, and others at the limit culminates in hate. Just as with anger, hatred admits of a natural and reasonable form: in this case, a willed aversion to evil and harmful things. Also, just as with anger, the kind of hatred relevant here opposes the reasonable form. The hatred in question is both excessive and directed against authentically good objects. Hatred forms an end state polar opposite to the natural love of God, self, and others that arises from participation, unity, and union; furthermore, this type of hatred opposes the supernatural love of God, self, and others that arises from charity's transformation of natural love.

Aquinas asks whether hatred should be counted among the deadly sins, since if it is opposed, and even directly opposed, to charity, it would seem to be even worse than the sources of sins already discussed. Simply stated, one might think that, if the virtues spring from love, then the vices must spring from hate. Aquinas responds that hate does indeed oppose love and charity, but because love comes first, hate must come last. The deadly sins with prideful self-love at their root slowly eat away at the good until no good remains, and hate fills the void where the love of the good should be.

Consequently it must first of all fail in that which is less in accordance with nature, and last of all in that which is most in accordance with its nature, since what is first in construction is last in destruction. Now that which, first and foremost, is most natural to man, is the love of what is good, and especially love of the Divine good, and of his neighbor's good. Wherefore hatred, which is opposed to this love, is not the first but the last thing in the downfall of virtue resulting from vice.[20]

As discussed in chapter 1, love forms the basis of all actions. Hatred, then, cannot be the ultimate cause of wrongdoing. However, it can be, and in fact is, the ultimate effect of wrongdoing.

In accordance with this, Aquinas reaffirms the kind of love that does cause sin— namely, disordered self-love. The pride-based estimation of one's own excellence produces an envious sorrow over

20. *ST* II-II, q. 34, a. 5.

all goods not exclusively belonging to oneself, which includes both the good of God and the goodness of one's neighbor. This sorrow persists through anger and then sloth. Finally, wishing to shun and avoid sorrow fully, the prideful person hates his neighbor as the purported cause of his own misery. "Hatred of his neighbor is a man's last step in the path of sin, because it is opposed to the love he naturally has for his neighbor."[21]

Love and hatred constitute something like transitive relations. The love of God makes possible and perfects the love of self, which in turn makes possible and perfects the love of others. Through disordered self-love, a person spurns and rejects God, which leads to further sin and vices. These vices further undermine and corrupt—cause further disorder to—the love of self, and thereby, further undermine and corrupt the ability and desire to love others. At the limit, the hatred of God feeds into an intense hatred of the parts of oneself most directly connected to God by way of participation. Fully disordered self-love, then, breeds hatred of one's neighbor insofar as a person relates to others as he relates to himself.

SATAN AND TEMPTATION

Before turning to Aquinas's account of appropriate conformity to the good and perfection of love, we should attend to one further consideration pertaining to the disordered love of self: demonic temptation. Aquinas spends considerable effort analyzing external influences that contribute to the perversion of love and its sinful effects. According to him, the three big sources of temptation are the world, the flesh, and the devil. The world tempts a person with the allure of money, prestige, and fame, while the flesh tempts with the promises of large quantities of sensual pleasure. These are largely impersonal forces. In contrast to this, devils, chiefly as led by Satan, are personal forces intentionally trying to pervert love in all three forms: God, self, and others.

---

21. *ST* II-II, q. 34, a. 6.

Aquinas asserts two key principles of demonic temptation: (1) Satan can influence bodily appetites and imagination; (2) he cannot manipulate reason itself. As a consequence of the second principle, he cannot literally cause a person to love inappropriately and sin.[22] Nonetheless, several passages in Aquinas paint a bleak picture in which a person's love of self stands vulnerable to Satan's influence, almost to the point of being at his mercy. In the *Commentary on Job*, Aquinas discusses the ability of human beings to combat Satan without God's aid. Since Satan exists as a superior kind of being, human beings lack the power to prevail in a matchup with him. In practical terms, this means that, without the active role of God, Satan will pervert a person's love of self to adapt to what is unsuitable, inevitably leaving the person unable to love others, isolated within oneself, and consumed with hate. At the limit, a person becomes a slave to Satan "by subjecting himself to him spontaneously."[23]

Aquinas's first point is that Satan cannot be overcome without the aid of God. Second, Aquinas identifies the susceptibility to Satan as a principal threat to everybody. Commenting on the conversation between God and Satan toward the beginning of the book of Job, Aquinas lays out the big picture of Job and human existence in terms of the wicked and good path available to all. Concerning the former, he states:

For since man is composed of a spiritual nature and of earthly flesh, man's evil consists in clinging to the earthly goods which belong to him by virtue of his earthly flesh after he has abandoned the spiritual goods towards which he is ordered by virtue of his rational mind. Therefore, evil men, inasmuch as they follow earthly nature, are rightly called earth. Satan, then, not only goes about such earth but also walks through it, because in earthly men he completes the effect of his malice.

---

22. *ST* I-II, q. 80, a. 3. Aquinas holds that Satan can effectively shut down a person's reason and have him do what he wants, but even here the person would not be sinning. The acts would not properly be coming from him but from Satan.

23. *ST* I-II, q. 80, a. 4, ad 2.

Addressing the nature of the good path, the same passage continues:

> For in walking through is designated the completion of the process itself, just as on the contrary it is said of just men that God walks among them.[24]

Finally, Aquinas emphasizes to those who follow the good path that their efforts in this life will always be imperfectly realized:

> And one should note that earthly affections imitate remotely in some way spiritual affections by which the mind is joined to God, but they can in no way arrive at a similarity with them. For earthy love, and consequently every affection, falls short of the love of God, for love is the source of any affection.[25]

The key implication relevant to the love of self is that a person does not direct his own self-love in the absence of the influence of a higher power, and there is more than one higher power.

If a person shuns God, he will cast his lot either explicitly or implicitly with Satan, who will incline the person toward increasingly perverted and disordered love of self. Such disordered self-love will ensure the impossibility of proper relationships and unions with others. Again, the self-preoccupation of sin leads to self-isolation, whereby a person lives deprived of the mutual indwelling afforded by friendship—he is cut off from the inner lives of others. On Aquinas's view, Satan strives to bring about such self-isolation and hatred through temptation insofar as it separates a person from God and other human beings. Conversely, if a person cultivates a loving relationship with God, his self-love becomes rightly ordered, which creates the proper conditions and motivation for entering into loving relations and friendships with others.

By way of perverting the appropriate ordering of love, Satan's malice performs an analogous, though inverse, role to God's love. Through a loving relationship with God, God orders and perfects

---

24. Aquinas, *The Literal Exposition on Job: A Scriptural Commentary Concerning Providence*, trans. Anthony Damico, interpretative essay and notes by Martin D. Yaffe (Atlanta, Ga.: Scholar's Press, 1989), 1:385–93.

25. Ibid., 1:434–40.

a person's self-love; relating to and uniting with Satan allows Satan to disorder and corrupt a person's self-love. Commenting on God's speech to Job speaking to the ultimate helplessness of the human being in relation to Satan, Aquinas discusses the variety of means for subjecting things to the human will and concludes that none of these apply to Satan. Due to this, human beings cannot overcome Satan through their own power.

> Having shown, then, that man cannot in any way by his own power overcome the devil, [God] concludes, as it were, from all that has been premised, adding *Put your hand upon him,* supply "if you can," as if to say: In no way by your own power can you put your hand upon him to subject him to you.[26]

If a human being cannot defeat and overcome Satan by his own power, then the cultivation of love toward communion with others and away from self-isolation is also not purely a function of the human will and reason.

Aquinas does not think the overall situation is hopeless. While a person cannot overcome Satan using his own power, God can defeat Satan and offers human beings the divine resources to do so. "But although [Satan] cannot be overcome by man, he is nevertheless overcome by divine power."[27] God offers such assistance to each person in the form of divine providence. Thus, providence provides a twin function. It takes on the role of not only providing goods, but also actively opposing destructive forces. God provides the means by which the deleterious effects of Satan's activities can be overcome.

Interestingly, the chief means is not a supernatural one, but rather a natural one in the form of the natural moral law. Supernatural principles then build upon the moral law. We considered the role of law in providence in chapter 3. God's providence over human beings includes bestowing on them the law by which to govern their own activity. As God leaves it up to each human being to govern himself,

---

26. Ibid., XL, 653–59.
27. Ibid.

each person, to avoid the deleterious effects of Satan and sin, must govern himself in the right manner. This is a self-governance not carried out as an end in itself, but as a means to love through conformity to God's law. Let us turn to the next chapter to treat these notions more fully.

5

The Fulfillment of Love in God

LOVE AND SELF-GOVERNANCE

This chapter examines the full perfection of the love of self in terms of what it requires, what it looks like, and how it benefits a person. I will focus first on self-governance—the ways of governing oneself through self-love—and then turn to how the possibility of union with others in friendship depends upon a self-governance rooted in proper love. The following section treats the particulars of how the natural love of God perfects self-love; the final section will treat the particulars of how the supernatural love of God perfects self-love. In the context of both the natural and supernatural love of God, we will look at how the perfection of the love of self though the love of God promotes and perfects the union with other human beings.

In *The Root of Friendship*, I discussed Aquinas's account of self-governance in terms of sustainability. Aquinas follows the long-established tradition of eudaimonism by holding that various ways of forming one's character boil down to two opposed trajectories. By failing to acquire virtue and allowing bodily desires and nonrational factors to grow too strong, a person loses the very ability to govern his own life. He becomes enslaved to his lower appetites, which neutralizes any substantive impact his reason and will can exercise in decision-making and action. On the other hand, by cultivating qualities allowing for self-governance—namely, the virtues serving to perfect one's motivational and epistemic powers—a person promotes long-term, sustainable self-governance.

Nonsustainable versus sustainable self-governance proves to be an important consideration for anyone who values self-governance. This becomes particularly the case when self-governance is situated in the larger context of love. We can state and then develop three principles concerning the relationship of love to self-governance. First, proper self-governance derives from love, especially self-love. Second, related to the first, the reason we should ultimately value self-governance is for the sake of love, particularly a loving union with God, a love-shaped interior life, and a loving union with other human beings. Thus, self-governance is not an end in itself, but rather a means to this end. Third, due to the first two principles, self-governance not tempered by proper love becomes a liability precipitating the self-preoccupation and self-isolation discussed in chapter 4.

Self-governance results from self-love. More precisely, two of the essential properties of the love of self form the activity of governing and directing one's own actions. Through self-love's properties of benevolence and beneficence, or more precisely the root of those properties as realized in the love of self, a person wills, pursues, and acquires goods for oneself and others. Thus, the condition of a person's self-love necessarily affects and shapes the quality of self-governance. In addition, because self-governance derives from self-love and is the means by which a person enters into a deeper relationship with God and cultivates loving unions with others, Thomistic self-governance differs in significant ways from the common contemporary notion of autonomy.

In my previous book, I made the case that Aquinas's account of self-governance satisfies the key desiderata of what contemporary thinkers tend to value in autonomy—namely, a person has the capacities to govern his own life and a rightful moral space in which to do so. Upon further reflection, I realize that I tried too hard to connect Kantian-inspired accounts of autonomy to Thomistic self-governance. I likely distorted some aspects of Aquinas's view to fit it into the modern framework. To avoid the same mistake, I have a more modest purpose in this section; I am aiming only to expand upon the connection between love and self-governance in Aquinas. I will not devote any space to argue for any affinity between Aquinas's view and other accounts, contemporary or otherwise.

For Aquinas, self-governance involves leading and directing oneself to the end of human existence. On the natural level, this end includes uniting oneself to God and union with others in friendship, while on the supernatural level, this end includes a mutual loving union with God in friendship and friendships with other persons on account of the divine friendship. We could summarize in four points the basic framework within which self-love extends to love of others. First, the most basic impulse of the will and the orientation of self-love is toward the whole good, particularly in terms of being united to God. Second, a person cannot will goods to himself without realizing he is committed by consistency to willing analogous goods to others like himself with whom he interacts. Third, the natural inclination of the love of self is toward love of others. Fourth, the love of friendship as willing the good to the other for his own sake leads to mutual friendships with others, which prove to be essential for a good, desirable life.

All these considerations point toward an understanding of self-governance that can equate neither to unrestrained willing nor to any notion of selfish willing. To see why, let us begin with the *Commentary on Matthew*, in which Aquinas considers four opinions concerning happiness—happiness as the possession of exterior things, the self-fulfillment of the will, active virtue, and contemplative virtue. The second opinion and Aquinas's rejection of it pertain most directly to the incompatibility of unrestrained willing and loving self-governance. The full opinion reads as follows:

Others [say] that perfect beatitude consists in the fact that a man fulfills his own will; hence we say, blessed is he who lives as he wants.... The will, which is twofold, according as it seeks two things: first that the will be forced by no higher law; second, that it be able to bind others as subjects: hence it desires to command, and not to be under another.[1]

Beatitude as the fulfillment of one's own will would amount to the ultimate selfish manner of willing—willing in a way unrestrained by anything other than one's own interests. Moreover, accompanying the desire for unrestrained willing is the aversion to any form of subjection to another. Aquinas rejects this account of beatitude precisely because it is inimical to love. By not conforming to the divine law, a person rejects a loving union with God and loving unions with other human beings. The activity of the will unconditioned by love seeks to create the artificial nonrelational identity previously discussed. In addition, as we saw, Aquinas contends that this sort of selfish activity terminates in self-isolation, misery, and hate.

In the *Commentary on the Nicomachean Ethics*, Aquinas expands upon the notion that selfish, wicked willing undermines the possibility of friendship. Unrestrained willing frustrates first the roots of the properties of beneficence, benevolence, and concord in the love of self, and then those same properties as found in interpersonal relationships.

[Aristotle] remarks first that bad men are at odds with themselves because they desire some pleasures agreeing with their sensitive appetite at the same time that they wish others agreeing with their reason. Such is obviously the case with the incontinent who want harmful pleasures instead of what they reasonably judge good. Thus they are doubly lacking in beneficence towards themselves: in one way, so far as they do what is harmful; in the other so far as they shun what it beneficial.[2]

Insofar as the wicked do not seek the good for themselves, they are in no position to seek it for others. Even if they knew how to seek the good for others, they would have no desire to do so. They lack benevolence, at the extreme, because they do not even really desire the good of their own existence. "So, since they have nothing in them-

---

1. Aquinas, *Commentary on the Gospel of Matthew*, 404 and 406.
2. Aquinas, *Commentary on Aristotle's Nicomachean Ethics*, 1814.

selves worth loving, they feel no love for themselves."³ "And they actually so flee from life that they sometimes do away with themselves."⁴ We see here the double-sided nature of the sword of consistency: good people, desiring to enhance their own existence and well-being, will goods to themselves and thereby will goods to others similar to them. The wicked, having no substantive desire to enhance their well-being, do not pursue goods for themselves and thus neither have reason to pursue goods for others.

Aquinas does maintain that even the wicked will seek the company of others; however, they cannot do so for reasons pertaining to the mutual pursuit of goodness and virtue. Consequently, there must be some other motive spurring on the wicked to congregation. In the context of discussing concord, Aristotle and Aquinas offer a suggestion for this motive by outlining two different reasons for seeking companionship. As treated in chapter 1, Aquinas's account of self-love involves considerations of the interior life—the heart. In the case of those with disordered self-love, their interior life is disordered and unpleasant.

On the other hand, the wicked have no wish to be preserved in the integrity of the inward man, nor do they desire spiritual goods for him, nor do they work for that end, nor do they take pleasure in their own company by entering into their own hearts, because whatever they find there, present, past and future is evil and horrible; nor do they agree with themselves, on account of the gnawings of conscience.⁵

In the previous chapter, we saw how sin causes intense sorrow. Sorrow, along with regret, strife, spite, and the general misery experienced within by the wicked, inclines them to flee from themselves. The last thing they want is to be alone with their own selves and their own thoughts. "But when they are in company they forget their wrong-doings in the distraction of external activities."⁶

---

3. Ibid., 1816.
4. Ibid., 1815.
5. *ST* II-II, q. 25, a. 7.
6. Aquinas, *Commentary on Aristotle's Nicomachean Ethics*, 1816.

The desire to flee from oneself toward others is a very different thing than love's natural tendency to extend outward. In the aforementioned instance, other people, at best, serve as a distraction to one's misery. Consequently, a miserable person does not even try to love the other with a love of friendship or go outside of himself in ecstasy to experience the inner lives of the others. Rather, he loves the other (if he loves others at all) solely with a love of concupiscence—the other represents a means of escaping his own tumultuous inner life, and so he wills the "good" of this escape. Such fleeing is produced from willed loneliness versus love.

We saw in the previous chapter another manifestation of wicked self-love: grasping more and more at the pleasures of wealth, food, drink, and sex to fill the void left by the absence of proper love of God, self, and neighbor. These pleasures also form a distraction or escape from one's own heart. As the desires for these pleasures grow increasingly immoderate, a person loses the ability to govern himself. Abilities necessary for self-governance, particularly the sensitive and rational appetites, must be properly cultivated to function well. The virtues, particularly courage, moderation, and justice, perfect these appetites and allow for sustainable, long-term self-governance. The vices, on the other hand, damage and virtually destroy the same abilities. Thus, as the vices increase, so a person's ability to govern himself decreases. A self-governance inimical to proper love leads to the vices, which in turn undermines the very ability to govern oneself.

Proper self-love promotes the virtuous cultivation of one's abilities, as such cultivation forms part of the true good of self. Moreover, the heart of the person with proper self-love lacks the discord and misery of the wicked. Thus, friends are not sought as a means of escape, but as an opportunity for sharing and mutual indwelling—giving oneself as a gift or good worth giving and receiving the other as a true good for oneself. The concord of friendship necessarily requires a basis in the good—willing the same sorts of goods that are truly perfective of human personal nature. Aquinas speaks to peace, particularly as the tranquility of order experienced within oneself, as deeper reality within oneself that manifests as concord between persons. "Concord denotes union of appetites among various persons, while peace denotes, in addition to union, the union of the appetites even in one man."[7] The person possessing well-ordered self-love is not beset by strife, regret, and misery. Rather, he has a peaceful inner life.

> They take pleasure in entering into their own hearts, because they find there good thoughts in the present, the memory of past good, and the hope of future good, all of which are sources of pleasure. Likewise they experience no clashing of wills, since their whole soul tends to one thing.[8]

In short, in terms of the relationship between proper self-governance and friendship, when a person marked by proper self-love seeks companionship, it is not to escape or flee oneself, but rather to share with or extend oneself to another. In addition, proper self-love provides the appropriate template for knowing how to love the other—willing and seeking true goods—and thus sustaining friendship in the long term.

Conversely, the deadly sins give rise to injustice—the perversion of one's rational appetite or will. In turn, this failure to love damages the possibility of sustainable self-governance. Justice, or treating others appropriately, pertains to the proper cultivation of the will supporting self-governance and love. This proper cultivation of the will, for Aquinas, begins in relation to God in the virtue of religion, which is connected or annexed to justice, as we saw in chapter 3. Let us turn to a closer look at how religion stabilizes and perfects self-love and thus contributes to the love of others.

LOVE AND WORSHIP

Thomistic self-governance constitutes the primary means to loving union with others and the joy resulting from resting in the good of

---

7. *ST* II-II, q. 29, a. 1.
8. *ST* II-II, q. 25, a. 7.

the beloved. The highest form of union is union with God, which in turn produces the most acute experience of joy flowing from it. Moreover, the proper union with God perfects self-love so as to make possible joyful unions with other human persons. Thus, we need to consider more fully the ways in which a person properly aligns himself to God and how these alignments serve to promote proper self-love and governance. Let us begin with the natural virtue of religion, through which a person unites himself to God through prayer, worship, and sacrifice. The next section treats the union with God through charitable friendship with him.

Joseph Pieper's work, *In Tune with the World: A Theory of Festivity*, offers a rich reflection on authentic festivity in terms of Aquinas's account of love, religion, and joy. Pieper's analysis serves as a nice point of departure for this section. He characterizes festivity as a free celebration. Instead of being tied to any practical goals, festivity springs from gratitude over one's existence as good. One of the marks of festivity is renunciation or sacrifice. Festivals do not exist for the sake of work; a person does not (or at least should not) celebrate to be a better and more productive worker. Rather, festivity is a sacrifice of utility and profit for the sake of something else.

The antithesis between holiday and workday, or more precisely, the concept of the day of rest, tells us something further about the essence of festivity. The day of rest is not just a neutral interval inserted as a link in the chain of workaday life. It entails a loss of utilitarian profit. In voluntarily keeping the holiday, man renounces the yield of a day's labor.[9]

A festival represents at least a limited disavowal of utility and material wealth for the sake of rejoicing. Pieper adds that only one motive makes possible such renunciation or sacrifice: love.

In terms of festive joy, Pieper affirms Aquinas's principle that joy results from the real possession of that which one loves. Accordingly, while festivals involve joy, the joy is a secondary phenomenon.

---

9. Josef Pieper, *In Tune with the World: A Theory of Festivity*, trans. Richard Winston and Clara Winston (South Bend, Ind.: St. Augustine's Press, 1999), 18. I thank Vincent Wargo for introducing me to this work and for our conversations about it.

A person cannot simply rejoice; he always rejoices over something. In turn, that over which he rejoices is the object of his love—joy is the response of a lover receiving what is loved. Finally, in the case of festive joy, one loves and affirms one's own existence and the world in which one lives. "Underlying all festive joy kindled by a specific circumstance there has to be an absolutely universal affirmation extending to the world as a whole, to the reality of things and the existence of man himself."[10] Again, "To celebrate a festival means: to live out, for some special occasion and in an uncommon manner, the universal assent to the world as a whole."[11]

As one moves from the straightforward affirmation of the goodness of both one's own existence and the existence of the whole world toward the source of the existence of oneself and the world, festivity becomes properly religious. Religious worship forms the greatest kind and most intense variety of festivity due to its metaphysical basis. Just as a loving affirmation of the world as good elicits joy and acts of rejoicing, a fortiori, a loving affirmation of the even greater goodness of the source of the world produces joy and acts of rejoicing. Pieper adds that religious worship becomes most intense in proportion to its ritualized, sacrificial nature. He contends that, just as a temple is a space set aside for the sake of worship, so the Sabbath forms a time set aside for worship. Thus, this time becomes sacred and foundational for religious ritual. By "sacrificing" the day's potential for utility and profit, a person is ushered into a mindset disposed toward festive worship.

While Pieper undoubtedly adds his own insight into the analysis, he draws heavily on the way Aquinas connects love to joy, worship, and, in a particular way, sacrifice. A person's metaphysical participation in God orients and draws his self-love toward love of God. The virtue of religion perfects his will to love God properly in this respect. Pieper uses the term "sacrifice" as an umbrella term under which falls what Aquinas specifies as essential acts of the virtue of re-

---

10. Ibid., 26.
11. Ibid., 30.

ligious worship—particularly devotion, prayer, sacrifice, and oaths. Pieper does a nice job of offering the big picture of how religious worship serves to perfect love and cause joy. Worship and sacrifice, as I am contending for Aquinas, also prepare the way for the proper love of neighbor. To establish this latter claim, let us take a closer look at the role worship plays in combating sin.

Sin causes sorrow over the good. Sorrow culminates in the hatred of neighbor, self, and God. To live a life of complete love, a person must overcome this sorrow. Aquinas draws attention to the need of conquering a particular deadly sin to begin the process—namely, sloth. Recall that sloth, at its root, is a lack of proper care or concern. Aquinas characterizes this lack of care in relation to the divine good indwelling within oneself. Turning this around, having a proper care or concern about the divine good in oneself rightly orders one in the depths of one's heart.

Love opposes sloth. Cultivating love, consequently, forms the obvious generic solution to conquering sloth. In terms of a more practical suggestion, Aquinas maintains that acts of worship combat and minimize sloth. We see this suggestion in the context of his response to a supposed objection that sloth cannot be a mortal sin. One of the necessary conditions for mortal sin is opposition to a given divine law, particularly as expressed in the Decalogue. Sloth does not seem to oppose any of the commandments directly; thus, it seems it cannot be a mortal sin. He replies by contending that sloth does oppose a commandment, particularly keeping holy the Lord's Day. He states:

> Sloth is opposed to the precept about hallowing the Sabbath-day. For this precept, in so far as it is a moral precept, implicitly commands the mind to rest in God: and sorrow of the mind about the Divine Good is contrary thereto.[12]

Through the natural impulse contained in the love of self, the heart of the person is oriented toward uniting oneself to God. Sloth frustrates the natural impulse and instead inclines one to shrink back

---

12. *ST* II-II, q. 35, a. 3, ad 1.

from one's ultimate metaphysical identity as participating in God and from those activities that are in accord with this relational identity.

In short, sloth dulls the love of God and replaces what should be the consequent joy of this love with a willed sorrow. Recovering the proper love of God begins with contemplating him. Affirmation and love of the source of one's existence prompt gratitude as well as the desire to set aside time to rest in that which one loves. The worship of God, including allowing one's mind to rest through contemplation and meditation in the divine presence, presents the most basic opportunity to develop this relationship through its integral acts of devotion, prayer, sacrifice, and oaths.

Devotion, "the will to do readily what concerns the service of God,"[13] disposes the will to conformity to the divine will. The next section extensively treats conformity and obedience, but it is enough to note that devotion constitutes one of the key interior acts of religion. The steadfast commitment to God as the highest good and source of one's own being directs the will rightly. Prayer forms the second act of religion. While full friendship with God cannot be obtained without charity, religion begins the process of uniting to God in friendship. Conversation is an essential mark of friendship, and prayer involves the beginnings of this exchange. In keeping with the cultivation of the will to love rightly, Aquinas speaks of prayer, particularly petitionary prayer, not as something that changes God's mind, but as an activity conforming the person to God. "For we pray, not that we may change the Divine disposition, but that we may impetrate that which God has disposed to be fulfilled by our prayers."[14] In keeping with the material nature of human existence, it is appropriate that sensible signs express the inward commitment of the will to God. Sacrifice and tithing perform this function. External forms of renouncing self-preoccupation and excessive attachment to material goods should be manifestations or expressions of a person's interior acts of the same nature.

---

13. *ST* II-II, q. 82, a. 1.
14. *ST* II-II, q. 83, a. 2.

As a person's self-love becomes properly ordered through religion, his reasons for sorrow and despair decrease, while occasions for joy increase. The analysis of Pieper points to how this dynamic becomes a motive undergirding the continual cultivation of religion. The connection between religion and joy forms a way by which religion disposes self-love to the proper love of others. If a person acts upon and cultivates his natural impulse to religion, he will experience a joy that can serve to neutralize the harmful acts of envy, anger, and sloth. First, joy acts an inoculation against self-preoccupation by disposing a person to experience others as part of the goodness of the world and not as competitors or threats. Second, religion teaches a person to sacrifice—to renounce one's own selfish interests for a greater good. A person relates to others as he relates to himself. Again, self-love is the template or model for how he relates to others. By acclimating oneself to sacrifice and forgoing immediate interests and an attachment to material goods, an unselfish person will be well-positioned to love others with a love of friendship. These first two considerations pertain to the love of God removing obstacles hindering the love of others. The third consideration focuses on the active role religion plays in promoting the love itself. Acts of religion incline a person to relate to others through love. Beginning with prayer, a person is to beseech God for bestowal of true goods on others, even one's enemies, because they are connected to one by way of similitude. The more the will conforms to God in religion (and charity), the more one loves others.

Along the same lines as prayer disposing one to the good of others, Aquinas considers oaths as essential to religion. Oaths invoke God as a guarantor to a commitment of some sort, either by way of declaring the seriousness of some matter or by promising future actions. These commitments usually involve other people. Thus, by swearing an oath, a person directs and disposes the movement of the will to proper relations with others. Aquinas does not treat oaths as ends in themselves, but as necessary remedies to disordered relations between persons.

Now an oath is required as a remedy to a defect, namely, some man's lack of belief in another man. Wherefore an oath is not to be reckoned among those things that are desirable for their own sake, but among those that are necessary for this life.[15]

For this reason, oaths should not be taken lightly or performed with great frequency. They are reserved for key moments in human relations where trust is at a premium. In this context, oaths serve to foster, maintain, and bolster proper love—the willing of true goods to others. A person lacking the virtue of religion, by extension, is thus inclined to perjury and the undermining of proper human relations.

To summarize, the virtue of religion habituates a person's will to love rightly. Without it, self-love tends to become disordered and self-preoccupied. When the latter happens, a person increasingly experiences others as a threat to his own excellence and as a competitor for material goods. At the limit, self-preoccupation culminates in self-isolation. Conversely, with religion, a person, first and foremost, conforms to a good greater than himself. Thus, religion combats wicked self-love at its root of prideful self-preoccupation. Uniting oneself to the whole good—that is, God—both serves as a cause of joy and directs one's actions outward toward the good of and union with others.

LOVE AND OBEDIENCE TO THE DIVINE WILL

In terms of proximate causality, proper self-love produces proper, loving self-governance. In terms of remote causality, self-love is proper—appropriately connected to the good—due to the love of God as rooted in participation in him. Thus, the love of God serves as a remote, and in this case ultimate, cause of a proper self-governance rooted in love. In the previous chapter, we discussed Aquinas's view that all actions necessarily involve conformity. Each time a person wills and acts, he is conformed or adapted to the object willed. Each act, then,

---

15. *ST* II-II, q. 89, a. 5.

constitutes, even if only slightly, a moment of self-determination. Moreover, from a long view, all of a person's actions throughout his life significantly determine the ability of his various capacities to function well, as well as the quality of his existence as a whole. Also, we have been treating how conforming to the wrong sorts of things leads one down the path of self-isolation and self-destruction. In this section, we will look at Aquinas's take on proper conformity to the divine will as the means for promoting the most loving and efficacious form of self-governance, which in turn effects the deepest loving unions and personal fulfillment.

Aquinas asks whether conformity to the divine will is necessary for goodness. In his affirmative response, he notes that, while each person naturally seeks the good, the complexities and competing interests of life make discerning the good difficult. As an illustration of such a situation, he considers a thief before a judge. The judge looks at the thief's moral wrongdoing and the harm inflicted on society, but the thief's wife focuses on the good of her family and how a sentence against her husband would inexorably harm this latter good. While the wife is right to consider the good of her family and the harm that would be inflicted upon it if her husband were put away, she is not looking to the more fundamental consideration of the common good. Aquinas's point is that particular goods must be related to the whole good.

> But a man's will is not right in willing a particular good, unless he refer it to the common good as an end: since even the natural appetite of each part is ordained to the common good of the whole. Now it is the end that supplies the formal reason, as it were, of willing whatever is directed to the end. Consequently, in order that a man will some particular good with a right will, he must will that particular good materially, and the Divine and universal good, formally.[16]

Thus, if a person seeks the good, all of his particular acts of willing of particular goods must be in line with or conformed to the divine will. As we saw in chapter 3, Aquinas contends that all particu-

---

16. *ST* I-II, q. 19, a. 10.

lar goods participate in the whole good, and the whole good is God. This participation is what makes the particular good a good in the first place. From an epistemic perspective, a person might not know the universal good is God, and consequently, he may not know that willing the whole good formally conforms him to the divine will. However, either way, the particular good refers to the whole good, and actions pertaining to the pursuit of the particular good must refer to the whole good to be appropriate. The divine will directs a person to refer the particular good to the whole good in the right way. In terms of the epistemological dimension, knowledge of the whole good amounts to knowledge of the divine will, particularly as expressed in the divine law. In terms of moral practice of conformity to the divine will, it occurs naturally through the virtue of religion and supernaturally through the virtue of charity.

Aquinas draws the strongest connection between conformity and the love of God in his account of divine friendship. In this context, he maintains that the property of friendship of concord must manifest itself as conformity to the divine law. Since human beings are fallible and limited, concord between human friends—the activity of willing and rejecting the same things—involves a give-and-take between them. Through mutual action, friends join their activities in the pursuit of an end. As infallible, God cannot join his will to the human will in the same way—there cannot be a give-and-take with perfection. Instead, the human being must conform his own will to God's in order to will and reject as God does. As Daniel Schwartz explains,

> Aquinas rightly calls our sharing the form of the divine will a "conformity" rather than a "unity" of wills, which is typically used to designate human concord. Unity of wills is a state of affairs that could be achieved by two persons modifying their wills so as to join a common cause, whereas conformity entails one person living up to a standard which itself remains fixed.[17]

---

17. Daniel Schwartz, *Aquinas on Friendship* (Oxford: Oxford University Press, 2007), 28–29.

Friendship with God involves concord with him, which in turn entails conformity to his will.

Aquinas further specifies that the means by which a person conforms to the divine will is obedience—namely, obedience to his commandments, which are an expression of his will for human beings.

> It is proper to friendship to consent to a friend in what he wills. Of course, the will of God is set forth for us by His precepts. Therefore, it belongs to the love by which we love God that we fulfill His commandments.[18]

Conformity to the divine good necessarily requires obedience to commandments. The commandments come in two forms: the natural moral law and further divine commands found in revelation. All of these commands, both natural and divine, are ordered to love. Commenting on the passage in Matthew, whereby Jesus affirms the two greatest commandments as love of God and neighbor as oneself and further adds that all other commandments depend upon these, Aquinas remarks:

> The teaching of the law and the prophets depends on these. The end in appetible things stand as do the principles in the speculative matters: for science proceeds from principles to conclusions, and in this way the whole science is judged from the principles, just as in all doable things the whole thing depends upon the end [which is love].[19]

In this passage and elsewhere, Aquinas consistently affirms two things: the necessity of obedience to moral precepts and the necessity of moral precepts to love. Love, particularly in terms of the union of possession, is the ultimate end of human action, and thus, everything else applicable to action, such as commandments and virtues, must be ordered to it. The loving union with God, first through religion and then by charitable friendship, constitutes the ultimate realizations of love. Obedience to divine commandments are both ordered to love and essential for it.

---

18. ScG IV, c. 22, p. 4.
19. Aquinas, *Commentary on the Gospel of Matthew*, 1820.

Obedience is usually not found among things contemporary thinkers count as positive ethical qualities. Indeed, many such thinkers likely dismiss what they take to be Aquinas's ethical account in large part because of his inclusion of obedience as a central virtue.[20] Yet, as is obvious, for Aquinas, we ought to value obedience precisely insofar as we value love. Accordingly, if love is among the things contemporary thinkers value, then a careful consideration of Aquinas's account is appropriate. To give Aquinas his full due, let us turn to his precise understanding of the nature of obedience and then examine its place in the love of God and love in general.

Aquinas classifies obedience as a virtue connected to justice. Through justice, a person gives to others what is due or owed to them. Obedience pertains to what a person owes a superior—namely, conforming one's will out of reverence to the will of the superior. Superiority comes in two forms: natural and circumstantial. As rational animals, adult persons generally are naturally equal with one another and naturally inferior to God.[21] However, on account of various offices and positions, some persons circumstantially possess a superior authority over others. Insofar as parents give their children existence, children are naturally inferior to them. Thus, adults naturally owe obedience to God and sometimes to other human beings, while children naturally owe obedience to their parents.

Since obedience involves the will conforming to the will of another as its principal act, it is properly a virtue pertaining to the will. However, determining *when* one ought to obey is a matter of reason. Thus, like all of the natural virtues for Aquinas, the practice of obedience falls under the virtue of prudence. Prudence, "right reason applied to action," perfects all of the activities associated with

---

20. For instance, Jerome B. Schneewind considers Aquinas's ethics to be a "morality of obedience" and as such contends that it does not satisfy contemporary desiderata for a viable ethical theory; Schneewind, *The Invention of Autonomy* (Cambridge: Cambridge University Press, 1998), 4.

21. For a good analysis of Thomistic equality and obedience, see Jean Porter, "Natural Equality: Freedom, Authority, and Obedience in Two Medieval Thinkers," *Annual of the Society of Christian Ethics* 21 (2001): 275–99.

reasoning about practical, moral matters. A prudent person inquires through counsel into the most appropriate course of action, judges from the information obtained, and acts.[22] A person should reason through all realistic options before acting. This process involves consulting one's own moral knowledge resulting from his past experience, apprehension of the good, and principles of the natural moral law connected to the pursuit of the good. In addition, he ought to seek the counsel of others if his own knowledge is incomplete. The final act of prudence is the command of the act judged to be the most fitting. Aquinas recognizes that the command of reason does not determine the person to act. It depends on the will as to whether and in what manner one finally acts. Thus, in the considered context, reason might judge and command an act of fitting obedience, but a will not cultivated by obedience—that is, a rebellious will—might nevertheless choose differently.

In short, a proper act of obedience requires the antecedent judgment of prudence, which Aquinas identifies with conscience. Only after a person has reasoned through the situation and found obedience to be appropriate should he conform his will to another's. Aquinas expresses this point when he addresses the inappropriateness of obedience to certain civil laws.

Laws may be unjust in two ways: first, by being contrary to human good ... either in respect of the end, as when an authority imposes on his subjects burdensome laws, conducive, not to the common good, but rather to his own cupidity or vainglory;—or in respect of the author, as when a man makes a law that goes beyond the power committed to him;—or in respect of the form, as when burdens are imposed unequally on the community, although with a view to the common good. The like are acts of violence rather than laws.... Wherefore such laws do not bind in conscience. Secondly, laws may be unjust through being opposed to the Divine good: such are the laws of tyrants including to idolatry, or to anything else contrary to the Divine law: and laws of this kind must nowise be observed.[23]

---

22. *ST* II-II, q. 47, a. 8.
23. *ST* I-II, q. 96, a. 4.

Obedience to another person's will is and ought to be an expression, and not a replacement, of self-governance. This is why blind obedience is never morally permissible. God exercises providence over human beings by creating the conditions for individual self-governance. If through reasoning a person determines that obedience in a given instance most conduces to his good, then he ought to conform his will to the other, whether this be to an individual person, a civil authority, or ultimately to God.[24]

Given love's supremacy in the ethical life for Aquinas, obedience is proper when it appropriately connects to love; otherwise it is not. Charity "directs the acts of all other virtues to the last end,"[25] which is principally the loving union with God in friendship and secondarily the loving union with other human beings. By being their ultimate form, charity entails all of the other natural and supernatural virtues. Thus, the perfect possession of charity is a sufficient condition for the possession of any given virtue.

To establish the point of the sufficiency of charity for obedience, Aquinas calls attention to the words of Jesus from John 14:23 that, if a person loves Jesus, one will obey and keep his commandments. He offers the following commentary on this passage:

Obedience follows from charity.... For the will, especially when it is concerned with an end, moves the other powers to their actions: for a person does not rest until he does those things which will bring him to his intended end, especially if it is intensely desired. And so, when a person's will is intent on God, who is its end, it moves all powers to do those things which obtain him. Now it is charity which makes one intent on God, and thus it is charity which causes us to keep the commandments.[26]

---

24. In terms of political obedience, Porter draws attention to Aquinas's notion of metaphysical equality as a limiting principle in legitimate obedience: "Aquinas makes explicit what Bonaventure only implies, namely, that the natural equality between persons limits the obligations of obedience"; Porter, "Natural Equality," 290.

25. *ST* II-II, q. 23, a. 8.

26. Aquinas, *Commentary on the Gospel of John*, trans. Fr. Fabian R. Larcher, OP, ed. Aquinas Institute (Lander, Wyo.: Aquinas Institute for the Study of Sacred Doctrine, 2013), 1942.

If a person possesses charity, he will obey appropriate commands in the right circumstances. Following the logic of sufficient conditionality, if X is a sufficient condition for Y, then Y is a necessary condition for X. Thus, the full possession of charity is a sufficient condition for the possession of virtuous obedience, and the full possession of obedience is a necessary condition for the full possession of charity.[27] Obviously, the fallen-ness of human nature rules out the perfect possession of either virtue in this life, but the relation between them captures both the template by which to understand them and the ideal to which a good person should strive.

In terms of obedience and friendship, in human relationships, if one person consistently seeks his own fulfillment at the expense of the other, there cannot be a friendship between them; since friendship requires benevolence and beneficence, complete selfishness destroys its possibility. Analogously, if a person follows his own will in opposition to the divine will, there cannot be a friendship with God. In the case of human relationships, human fallibility might occasion the reasonable resistance to pursuing that which a friend pursues. If the beloved seeks something objectively harmful, then a person's proper self-love mandates willing a different end or course of action. In this instance, the lover has good reason to resist full concord. However, God's perfection eliminates this problematic in divine friendship. Thereby, for Aquinas, a human lover lacks any reason from goodness to resist conformity to God's will. In short, obedience to divine commands is always appropriate in the context of a loving union with God.

Addressing the place of obedience in the context of the virtue of religion in comparison to charity, Aquinas notes that in religion, a

---

27. Aquinas's distinction between infused and acquired virtue makes this claim a bit simplistic. However, it works for our general purposes and is in keeping with his approach of examining the perfect instance of a thing (in this case, fully realized human existence) as the proper means of understanding it. In the *Commentary on the Gospel of John*, 2012, he remarks that obedience to the divine commandments "is not the cause of divine friendship but the sign, the sign that both God loves us and that we love God." The cause of divine friendship ultimately is "the gratuitous choice of God"; ibid., 2019.

person's motives to be religious and to act religiously always involve an element of what he calls "servile fear." Fear comes in two different varieties: "For there are two kinds of fear: servile fear, which casts out love ... and filial fear, which is generated out of charity."[28] Servile fear is the fear a slave has toward the master. It involves at least an implicit threat of punishment. Filial fear is the reverence one has toward an esteemed loved one—for instance, one's parents. Out of reverence and not wanting to let his parents down, a person does what they ask of him. Love of the other forms the chief cause of filial fear, while with servile fear, love of self, in terms of fear of punishment, factors heavily into the cause of servile fear. With religion, acts such as prayer and devotion tend toward reverence. However, since religion is fundamentally asymmetrical—human beings striving for God—it never completely casts out servile fear of its own nature.

Aquinas carefully notes that the kind of obedience found in divine friendship is not rooted in servile fear. Instead of a master/slave relationship, divine friendship is based upon a father/son relationship. A slave acts not of his own accord, but for the master's sake, and the master does not relate to the slave for the sake of the slave, but for his own sake. A son, while respecting the father's will, acts for his own accord, and the father relates to the son for the sake of the son. In short, a son of God is free. God does not use the human person, for he loves him for his own sake, and he is free to act on his own judgment.

Aquinas speaks to this in terms of the effects of the Holy Spirit dwelling within the person in friendship. When the Holy Spirit prompts human action, he does so nonviolently and in such a way as to free one from fear:

> But the Holy Spirit so inclines us to act that He makes us act voluntarily, in that He makes us lovers of God. Therefore, the sons of God are impelled by the Holy Spirit freely out of love, not slavishly out of fear.... Therefore, since the Holy Spirit inclines the will by love toward the true good, to which the will is naturally ordered, he removes both that servitude in

---

28. Aquinas, *Commentary on the Gospel of John*, 2015.

which the slave of passion infected by sin acts against the *order* of the will, and that servitude in which, against the movement of his will, a man acts according to the law, its slave, so to say, not its friend.[29]

A friendship with God casts out slavish obedience in favor of loving obedience. Thereby, virtuous obedience to God increases a person's freedom from servile fear and increases his ability to love both God and others with a love of friendship.

The upshot of Aquinas's distinction between servile fear and love is that obedience to divine commandments is necessary, both for a proper love of God and for loving self-governance, which is rooted in proper self-love. Aquinas clarifies this as he wrestles with the text of John, whereby Jesus affirms that his disciples are not servants, but friends. Aquinas wishes to preserve the superiority of God in friendship, and thus a kind of servitude. However, he also wishes to affirm a substantive meaning to Jesus's words. He begins with the previously mentioned distinction between fear and love, but now adds a third layer: being a son of God requires a kind of good servitude compatible with friendship.

There is a difference between the actions of servants and of free men, because the servant acts by the cause of another; the free, however, acts as a cause of himself, as much the final cause of the work as the moving cause.... But it sometimes falls to a servant to act by the cause of another, as the final cause [as if in cooperation]; still, he acts by himself, insofar as he moves himself to work: and this is good servitude, because it is moved out of charity to the doing of good works.[30]

With these points, Aquinas adds an additional layer to his analysis of self-governance proceeding from proper self-love, as informed by the love of God.

In chapter 4, we saw that wicked self-love leads to self-preoccupation and culminates in self-isolation and hatred. Through any action, a person conforms to the object sought. If these objects are inappropriate, it leads to an increasingly disordered love of self and

29. *ScG* IV, c. 22, p. 5–6.
30. Aquinas, *Commentary on the Gospel of John*, 2015.

interior wretchedness. Proper self-love—the love of self as perfected by the love of God—inclines a person to appropriate activity. A friend of God acts freely in the absence of fear, but the free acts are in cooperation with God's moving power. The final cause of proper self-love is union with God and proper union with others. God sets these ends with the love of charity, but a person must be free to perform actions within those parameters to secure these goods. In effect, a person cannot be forced to be friends with God, his own self, or anyone else; he requires the freedom to seek the good actively and will the good to others.

Let us conclude this chapter with a look at how Aquinas contends that the love of self, perfected by charity, extends to love of others. Charity perfects the will. The charitable will is habitually responsive to God as the whole good and source of all perfection. It serves to perfect the unity of the person to the highest degree possible. At the natural level, religion mitigates, and at the limit, eliminates the self-preoccupation that leads to self-isolation. At the supernatural level, charity builds upon and perfects this proper ordering of love, first toward God, then self, and finally neighbor. Through charity, a person experiences God not as a distant, fully transcendent entity to be feared, but ultimately as a friend. As the mutual indwelling with human friends causes a joyful delight, even more does the mutual indwelling with the perfect source of one's existence. Also, just as religion prepares the way and encourages loving unions with others, even more does charity.

The principal act of charity is love of God and, secondarily, the love of all people as related to God. A person has a greater cause for love of others with charity because charity unites all human beings to a common good. Since the charitable love of neighbor derives from the love of God, it takes on a greater fervor and open-endedness relative to natural love alone. In effect, through charity, the love of neighbor passes through, so to speak, the love of God. In so doing, the love of God transforms the love of neighbor from its natural state into something more substantive in a couple ways.

There is no limit to the will's desire and resting in God. Since God is an infinite good, the will finds continuing satisfaction through loving him. While other human beings are finite goods, God's relation to them communicates a share of this open-endedness. What begins with nature with the natural union of similitude is elevated and perfected by grace—namely, the similitude of all being, by nature, personal creatures of God, and, by grace, children of God. Moreover, love begets love. The more one seeks the good and desires union with another, the more the love as love grows. Provided that impediments to love are avoided and forces contrary to love suppressed, love will naturally increase.

In the *Commentary on John*, Aquinas calls attention to an important mark of the love of charity with respect to other human beings: mutuality. Commenting on the words of Jesus commanding that "you love one another, as I have loved you," Aquinas notes that this goes beyond, in a sense, loving one's neighbor as oneself solely with benevolence.

> It is the very nature of friendship that it is not imperceptible; otherwise, it would not be friendship, but merely good-will. For a true and firm friendship the friends need a mutual love for each other; for this duplication makes it true and firm. Our Lord, wanting there to be perfect friendship among his faithful and disciples, gave them this command of mutual love.[31]

The love of self as perfected by the love of God in charity tends not merely toward benevolence and even beneficence but full union with others, particularly those with similarly perfected love of self.

This is also the case for a person's self-love. As a person is related to God, he should love himself fervently by willing the good to himself out of the love of God. Just as the love of God elevates the union of similitude between persons, so the same grace perfects one's substantial unity as rooted in God by participation. Thereby, the grace contributes to the full integration of the self. Finally, proper self-love

---

31. Ibid., 1837.

will lead to stronger and more resolute love of self with a more intense and delightful interior life.

To summarize, for Aquinas, each human being conforms to what he wills. By eschewing the love of and real union with God, the trajectory of his willing will be toward self-preoccupation. Self-preoccupation leads to a miserable self-experience dominated by a willed sorrow—sorrow over the good of one's neighbor and sorrow over failing to acquire true goods—and an increased domination of sense appetites over rational choice. Both of these trends undermine the possibility of the love of friendship and union with others. Thus, self-preoccupation culminates in self-isolation. On the other hand, through a softening of one's heart "to be ready for the entrance of the beloved,"[32] a person becomes receptive to the love of God. Loving the greater good of God fulfills his nature as a being related to God metaphysically through participation. Through the divine law, the proper love of God cultivates a proper love of self. As the love of others depends upon and is shaped by self-love, the proper love of self extends outward to the proper love of and communion with others.

---

32. *ST* I-II, q. 28, a. 5.

6

The Love of Self and Subjectivity

THE LOVE OF SELF AND CONSCIOUS SELF-EXPERIENCE

In *The Root of Friendship*, I argued that Aquinas includes a notion like subjectivity in his account of the person and treats it as a central element within his anthropology. As stated in the introduction, my hope in this book is to develop this argument, but to do so in a way that allows for a standalone, systematic study of Aquinas's account of the connections between participation, unity, and union and how they serve as the foundation for and shape the orientations of the love of God, love of self, and love of others. Thus, even if the reader is not convinced of my argument for Thomistic subjectivity, he or she may still find useful the preceding five chapters analyzing unity and love. This chapter turns to subjectivity. I hope it is not presupposed within the previous chapters. Nonetheless, I do think it a natural continuation of them.

In terms of subjectivity, we find two (nonexclusive) principal characterizations of it in contemporary thought. The first is subjectivity as the ongoing conscious experience of oneself as subject. A good representative of this view is Karol Wojtyla.[1] I will call this

---

1. For a look at his view, see Karol Wojtyla, "Subjectivity and the Irreducible in the

"experiential" or "interior" subjectivity, as it speaks to personal inwardness and the experience of one's self. I take Charles Taylor to be speaking to the same basic notion in his studies of the historical development of the notion of selfhood.[2] Interestingly, both thinkers explicitly deny that Aquinas has a concept in any way approximating to subjectivity. Wojtyla argues that the Aristotelian/Thomistic definition of man as rational animal, which he takes as representative of Aquinas's anthropology, is too "cosmological" and not sufficiently "personalistic." He maintains that this definition fails to account for the nature and importance of subjectivity. Taylor, for his part, contends that the history of the notion of subjectivity effectively begins with Descartes, mentioning the ancients and giving a passing nod to Augustine. Aquinas does not even form part of his narratives.

The second understanding of subjectivity, which I will term "irreducible subjectivity," relates to the subjectivity as the conscious experience of oneself, but pushes a bit further by affirming its irreducibility with other persons' analogous experience. Linda Zagzebski offers the following description, along with a claim of its nonancient or nonmedieval origins:

> Subjectivity is consciousness as it is experienced by the individual subject. At some point in the modern era, philosophers began to appreciate that the viewpoint of the individual subject cannot be reduced to an alleged objective viewpoint outside any person's consciousness ... if persons are unique, as I believe they are, a primary candidate for their uniqueness is their unique perceptual perspective, and even more fundamentally, the uniqueness of contents of their consciousness.[3]

Each person has the conscious experience of himself as subject, but the experience is fundamentally unique and nonreducible to the experience of others.

Human Being," in *Person and Community: Selected Essays*, trans. Theresa Sandok, OSM (New York: Peter Lang, 1993), 209–17.

2. Charles Taylor, *Sources of the Self: The Making of the Modern Identity* (Cambridge, Mass.: Harvard University Press, 1989), and Taylor, *A Secular Age* (Cambridge, Mass.: Belknap Press of Harvard University Press, 2007).

3. Linda Zagzebski, "Omnisubjectivity: Why It Is a Divine Attribute," *Nova et Vetera* 14, no. 2 (2016): 435.

In *The Root of Friendship*, without making this distinction, I focused on interior over irreducible subjectivity. I contend that we can make a strong case for Thomistic subjectivity in both senses. It is easier to make the case for interior subjectivity, but my argument for it suggests that something like irreducibility is also built into Aquinas's understanding. Fortunately, I am not alone with my claim that subjectivity forms an important dimension of Aquinas's account of the person. An expanding body of scholarship focuses on self-knowledge and subjectivity in Aquinas, scholarship that I do not hesitate to commend as superior to my own.[4]

In *Aquinas on Human Self-Knowledge*, Therese Scarpelli Cory lays out a strong case for Aquinas's inclusion of what I am calling "experiential subjectivity" in his account.

[These cited passages from Aquinas] reveal what phenomenon Aquinas is seeking to explain: namely, self-awareness is an ordinary, first-personal awareness of myself, my own existence, my mental acts. Aquinas generally conveys this intimate, first-personal character with the reflexive pronouns *se* and *seipsam*. But in some instances, he even adopts the first-person perspective of the self-knower: "I understand myself to understand," equating such personal self-understanding with cognition of one's own intellect: "We do not cognize our intellect except insofar as we understand ourselves to understand." Self-awareness is simply an everyday concrete prephilosophical experience of oneself, and not some detached philosophical endeavor to examine "the I."[5]

On her interpretation, Aquinas's view of self-knowledge involves several points of description, one of them being "habitual self-awareness is the mind's very self-presence pre-dating all cognitive acts."[6] She conducts her analysis by first offering Aquinas's "quasi-phenomeno-

---

4. Norris Clarke, SJ, stands out as a scholar placing subjectivity at the heart of a Thomistic anthropology, although he often understands himself as offering a "creative completion" of Aquinas versus a straight interpretation of Aquinas; see especially Clarke, *Person and Being* (Milwaukee: Marquette University Press, 1993).

5. Therese Scarpelli Cory, *Aquinas on Human Self-Knowledge* (Cambridge: Cambridge University Press, 2014), 70–71. The two citations from Aquinas are, respectively, *Scriptum super libros Sententiarum* I, 1.2.1, reply 2, and *Sentencia libri De amina* III.3.

6. Cory, *Aquinas on Human Self-Knowledge*, 116.

logical" account of what self-knowledge and self-awareness are and then turns to a detailed account of how such notions are possible, given Aquinas's broader philosophical commitments, particularly his views on cognition.[7] For the most part, I will not be attempting the latter task, other than to show in general terms how Thomistic subjectivity is nested within his underlying commitment to the relationship between metaphysical participation in God and personal substantial unity. Instead, I will direct my efforts to showing that Aquinas has an account of experiential and irreducible subjectivity based upon his notion of the love of self and that these are central to his notion of personhood.

In terms of Aquinas's distinctions within self-love, I contend that common self-love constitutes the basis for a person's ongoing experience of oneself as subject.

Love of self is common to all, in one way; in another way it is proper to the good; in a third way, it is proper to the wicked. For it is common to all for each one to love what he thinks himself to be. Now a man is said to be a thing, in two ways: first, in respect of his substance and nature, and, this way all think themselves to be what they are, that is, composed of soul and body. In this way too, all men, both good and wicked, love themselves, in so far as they love their own preservation.[8]

Common self-love constitutes the basis for subjectivity. "Proper self-love" is common self-love properly oriented to the good, while "improper self-love" is the same root love directed away from the good.

To lay the groundwork for my argument, let us revisit Aquinas's use of the term "heart." He characterizes the union of friendship as that which makes "one heart of two." The heart constitutes the deepest interior of the person. In his scriptural commentaries, he interprets passages having to do with the interior life as referring to the heart. For instance, speaking to the Christ finding a man he cured of infirmity in the temple, Aquinas notes:

7. Mark K. Spencer offers a similar sort of argument, defending subjectivity as coherent within an Aristotelian framework; Spencer, "Aristotelian Substance and Personalistic Subjectivity," *International Philosophical Quarterly* 55, no. 2 (2015): 145–64.
8. *ST* II-II, q. 25, a. 7.

We see from this that this man was not cured in vain, but having been converted to a religious way of life, he visited the temple and found Christ: because if we desire to come to the knowledge of the Creator, we must run from the tumult of sinful affections, leave the company of evil men, and flee to the temple of the heart, where God condescends to visit and live.[9]

The heart is so named because it involves three things: affections, depth, and centrality. It is the deepest part of the person, where the person experiences most acutely his own thoughts, desires, and affections, particularly consolation and joy. Clearly, it is an important aspect, if not the most central aspect, of personal identity for Aquinas. It represents the core of who a person is—a core encountered in love of God and that which is loved in others through intimate friendship.

I contend that the heart represents at the experiential level what incommunicability is at the metaphysical level. More precisely, I think the heart forms the most acute subjective experience of one's own personal incommunicability. In the following passage, we see Aquinas drawing upon and expanding Boethius's characterization of personhood.

Accordingly we reply that the term person signifies nothing else but an individual substance of a rational nature. And since under an individual substance of a rational nature is contained the substance, individual, i.e. incommunicable and distinct from others, whether of God, of man, or of angels, it follows that a divine Person must signify something subsistent and distinct in the divine nature, just as a human person signifies something subsistent and distinct in human nature: and this is the formal signification of a person whether divine or human.[10]

"Person" denotes something individual over and above the communicable nature of a thing, and personal incommunicability takes on special significance, since it individualizes rationality.[11] Such sub-

---

9. Aquinas, *Commentary on the Gospel of John*, 730.
10. Aquinas, *On the Power of God*, q. 9, a. 4.
11. It is probably clear from the context, but given Wojtyla's critique of the definition of man as rational animal, it is worth emphasizing that Aquinas does specify that "rationality" is not being used in the restricted sense of moving from propositions to a conclusion. Rather, he intends an inclusive broad sense including all powers and operations of

sistent, incommunicable beings of a rational nature constitute the apex of being itself. Aquinas maintains that *"person signifies what is most perfect in all nature—that is, a subsistent individual of a rational nature."*[12] He elaborates that such a being possesses a dignity found in nothing else.

> Thence by some the definition of person is given as *hypostasis distinct by reason of dignity*. And because subsistence in a rational nature is of high dignity, therefore, every individual of the rational nature is called a *person*.[13]

The heart is the deepest subjective self-experience of this metaphysical uniqueness and dignity. I argue that the love of self serves as the foundation for subjective self-experience in general and, by extension, at the deepest level the heart. To make this case, I will review and then draw upon some of the key notions from chapter 1.

Most properly, love is an act of the will involving the unions of similitude, affections, and possession. An individual's love for himself proceeds from his own substantial union or unity. In the case of two things, something more than unity is required, as two things cannot form a unity in a literal sense. If the persons seek a relationship with one another, we have a union of affection. This second union is the affective bond within which the lover relates to the beloved as another self. Finally, the affective bond between the lovers tends toward the union of possession or real union with each other. Real union between persons involves both mutual presence and the indwelling in the interior of each other.

As we have seen throughout this text, Aquinas emphasizes the priority of the love of self over the love of others precisely due to the relationship between unity and union.

---

our intellectual nature. Further commenting on Boethius's definition of person, he states, "*Rational* is the difference of animal, inasmuch as *reason* whence it is taken denotes discursive knowledge, such as is in angels but not in man nor in God. But Boethius takes *rational* in a broad sense for *intellectual*, and this is common to man, angels and God"; Aquinas, *On the Power of God*, q. 9, a. 2, ad 10.

12. *ST* I, q. 29, a. 3.
13. *ST* I, q. 29, a. 3, ad 2.

We must hold that, *properly speaking, a man is not a friend to himself, but something more than a friend*, since friendship implies union, for Dionysius says (*Div Nom*. iv) that "love is a unitive force," whereas a man is one with himself which is more than being united to another. *Hence, just as unity is the principle of union, so the love with which a man loves himself is the form and root of friendship*. For if we have friendship with others it is because we do unto them as we do unto ourselves, hence we read in *Ethic*. ix. 4, 8, that "the origin of friendly relations with others lies in our relations to ourselves."[14]

Self-love is greater than love of others because the metaphysical bases from which each proceed determine that such must be the case. Union derives from unity. The love based on unity, self-love, must be greater than the love based on union, love of others.

Moreover, the development and direction of self-love shapes how a person relates to others, as each person relates to others as he relates to himself. Aquinas uses the notion of friendship as the paradigm of love between persons, which he then employs to flesh out self-love. Friendship is the habitual love between two people in which each individual wills and seeks goods for the other. Moreover, the key dimension of the love of friendship is that the friend loves the beloved as a subject or person.

As it involves willing and seeking goods for oneself, the love of self is structurally prior to friendship, or to use Cory's term, self-love "predates" friendship. We saw how Aquinas articulates the nature of proper self-love in terms of the properties of friendship: longing, benevolence, beneficence, pleasure, and concord. The properties we find in a healthy friendship result from basic dimensions of a person's love of self. In terms of the property of longing in a friendship between persons, there is a metaphysical separation of substances; hence, a person longs to be with and to be united to the beloved (the union of affection and union of possession, respectively). In self-love, there is no metaphysical separation, though the love can be directed to different aspects of oneself. When self-love is proper, a person relates most fundamentally to his inward nature as an in-

---

14. *ST* II-II, q. 25, a. 4.

communicable person versus predominately toward his own nonrational characteristics.

The roots of benevolence and beneficence in self-love concern willing and seeking true goods enhancing both one's nature and the integrity of one's interior life. Thus, the activity of self-governance itself derives from self-love. In friendship, pleasure and concord relate to the experiential dimension of the other. Self-love is the form (*forma*) and root (*radix*) of friendship. Each person relates to others in a manner shaped and informed by how he relates to himself. Thus, proper self-love forms a key condition for both developing a true friendship and nurturing and sustaining the friendship over time.

Going one step further, the following represents the key principle in which we find Aquinas relating self-love to something like a person's ongoing self-experience: "Just as unity is the principle of union, so the love with which a man loves himself is the form and root of friendship." The relationship between proper self-love and friendship allows for what I call the "primacy of self-love principle" —namely, since friendship derives from proper self-love, anything that is known about friendship can be predicated, mutatis mutandis, of proper self-love.

Given that the experience of friendship includes the conscious and intimate experience of the beloved, self-love, especially as appropriately developed in proper self-love, must involve the conscious experience of oneself. Aquinas's account of the role of unity and union in love further contributes to the legitimacy of this interpretation. The union of similitude allows for the unions of affection and possession of friendship. As self-love does not arise from union, but from unity, the experience of self-love is more basic and stronger relative to the conscious experience of the other in friendship. Complete friendship between persons involves the habitual (and mutual) love of friendship. Each friend is disposed to will and seek goods for the other and to desire further conscious union with the other. The self-experience of self-love must then go beyond the habitual. It is not a disposition, but an ongoing self-experience.

Cory makes the analogous point, I think, when she discusses what it means to say that self-presence is habitual. She carefully notes that "habitual" does not, in this case, refer to a habit, but "rather, the essence of the soul *is functionally parallel to a habit for actual self-awareness.*"[15] The essence of the soul is or involves the disposition to self-presence in its activity.

In fact, since it is intellectual, the soul's *being itself* entails its natural *presence to itself*. But this self-presence is just a "first perfection" or "equipped state" in which the intellect is already essentially disposed to cognize itself. *The human soul, then, cannot be intellectual without also being "pre-equipped" for self-awareness.* The same idea can be rephrased in terms of the ontology of the human soul. Because the human soul is intellectual, its ontological self-identity is a cognitive self-presence (a habitual self-awareness).[16]

In friendship, the conscious experience of the inner life of a friend is a derivative reality. It can be intimate, intense, and through mutual indwelling, reach to the heart of the beloved's interior life. The self-experience of proper self-love, though, is the root reality. It simply is the continuous experience of oneself containing the full depth of interiority.

One might object that I am placing too much emphasis on the will in relation to self-knowledge. For instance, it is clear from the Cory passages that she is speaking directly to the intellect. I think she is right to do so. For Aquinas, the will is not the intellect and by its own nature does not know anything. However, my claim is this: self-love is the principal and primary cause of self-experience, but human self-love inevitably "runs through" the intellect, giving subjectivity the character it does. We see this if we take a step back and notice that self-love is central to all beings for Aquinas. All beings, all substances, love themselves as their first act. "There is a union which causes love; and this is substantial union, as regards the love with which one loves oneself.[17] This natural love, *amor*, forms the basis of

---

15. Cory, *Aquinas on Human Self-Knowledge*, 124.
16. Ibid., 128.
17. *ST* I-II, q. 28, a. 1, ad 2.

self-preservation and other natural instincts and inclinations. In human substances, the love involves choice, *dilecto electiva*, which naturally then involves the intellect. Consequently, this fundamental relation of self-love proceeding immediately from substantial unity as the latter's first act transforms into personal self-experience for substances of a rational nature.

Thus, what I am calling self-love (and what I think Aquinas means, given his further statements on it) begins in the will and serves as the root cause of a self-experience involving the intellect (and sense powers). This use of the term concerns a straightforward analogy to how Aquinas addresses friendship. Friendship includes more than the will. It is an experiential reality involving the senses, affections, and intellect, which we saw with the extensive list of properties Aquinas predicates to it. However, at its root, Aquinas identifies friendship principally with the will. Friendship, first and foremost, is a kind of love, and as the kind of love it is, it serves as the basis for all of the other dimensions of friendship.

I define proper self-love as the appropriate development of a person's immanent love as directed toward oneself as an incommunicable subject/person and articulate five of its essential properties in the following manner. In terms of self-love, longing takes the form of the preservation of one's interior life. The roots of benevolence and beneficence involve the desiring and seeking of goods that contribute to one's own flourishing. The roots of pleasure and concord relate to the affective dimension of self-experience—namely, the delight and pleasure produced by entering into one's heart and the internal peace and concord resulting from an integrated interior life.

As the self-experience of self-love flows immediately from personal substantial unity, it is structurally prior to and grounds the possibility of further experience. Stated differently, personal self-experience is the subjective pole in the subject/object relation of experience and action. Moreover, in terms of an irreducible character of subjectivity, which the next section will take up more fully, as a person relates to his own incommunicableness and distinctness in self-love, the experience must be irreducible relative to other human beings. Each person has his own incommunicable conscious self-experience. This is the difference between unity and union at the subjective level. Ontological unity entails a thing being what it is and does not share its being with another. Each person has his own unique subjective self-experience deriving from personal unity. Thus, conscious self-experience is irreducible to another person's self-experience, and so on with every human person. Moreover, all consequent perception experience, as grounded upon and an extension of personal self-experience, takes on the same irreducible character.

PARTICIPATION, IRREDUCIBILITY, AND OMNISUBJECTIVITY

Based on the human person's participation in God and human subjectivity deriving from self-love, we can give an argument that God's omniscience entails omnisubjectivity. In laying out the case for this, we will also give a more detailed argument to the conclusion that Thomistic subjectivity has at least a quasi-irreducible character. In terms of my argument, I am both drawing upon and responding to Zagzebski, who has recently offered compelling defenses of the importance and coherency of the concept of divine omnisubjectivity.

She makes the case that omnisubjectivity should be included among the key attributes ascribed to God. She defines omnisubjectivity as "the property of consciously grasping with perfect accuracy and completeness every conscious state of every creature from that creature's first-person perspective."[18] She argues for the importance of this attribute, noting that it seems supremely fitting as a divine property. In addition, she briefly discusses its compatibility with the philosophical theology of Aquinas. However, on her view, Aquinas does not have an account of human subjectivity and thus does not

18. Linda Zagzebski, *Omnisubjectivity: A Defense of a Divine Attribute* (Milwaukee: Marquette University Press, 2013), 10.

The Love of Self and Subjectivity

treat anything like omnisubjectivity. As mentioned in the previous section, she defines subjectivity as "consciousness as it is experienced by the individual subject."[19]

Zagzebski argues that the traditional conception of divine omniscience in general and Aquinas's understanding in particular fail to account for God's knowledge of each person's own subjective perspective. Thus, there is room to add the property of omnisubjectivity to the list of properties God possesses. Moreover, traditional religious activities such as prayer seem to presuppose and require that God is capable of understanding what it is like to be human—to grasp each person's own subjective experience from that person's first-person perspective. Therefore, there is an appropriateness to adding the property to an understanding of God.

Speaking to why omniscience is insufficient to capture this dimension of the divine nature, she notes:

> How can a divine being know what it is like to be one of his creatures? No traditional Christian denies that God knows all the objective facts about his creation.... The problem is that knowing all the facts about his creatures is not enough to know everything there is to know about his creatures because there is more to know about them than the facts. Having conscious states is a feature of conscious beings.... If God knows everything, he must know the subjective part of his creation as well as the objective facts.[20]

In terms of interpreting Aquinas, Zagzebski is not denying that he includes omniscience in his account, but only that omniscience alone fails to capture what she means by omnisubjectivity.

Affirming the idea that God knows the subjective part of his creation leads to a question of whether the notion of omnisubjectivity itself is consistent. How could God actually understand things from another person's first-person perspective when he is not that person? Omniscience entails that, if Mary sees in color, then God knows that Mary sees in color. However, omnisubjectivity requires that God

---

19. Zagzebski, "Omnisubjectivity: Why It Is a Divine Attribute," 435.
20. Ibid., 437.

knows what it is like to see in color and that he knows what it is like for Mary to experience color consciously. Zagzebski argues that we can use the notion of empathy to understand how God knows another person's first-person perspective.

In instances of human empathy, the empathizer imagines what it would be like to experience what the other person is undergoing. This enables him to feel as if he himself were in the same situation. Drawing on the structure of empathetic experience, Zagzebski posits the notion of total empathy to explain how God could experience a human person's subjective experiences. "I propose that God has total perfect empathy with all conscious beings who have ever lived or ever will live."[21] Perfect empathy allows God to experience everything Mary experiences, but Mary's experiences remain her own. "Since your state is from your first-person point of view, God grasps it from your first-person point of view, but in an empathic way, never forgetting that he is not you."[22]

In terms of Aquinas, Zagzebski argues for the compatibility of her view with his. She contends that Aquinas's notion of divine omnipresence, combined with omniscience and omnipotence, is consistent with something like omnisubjectivity. However, in terms of the notion of subjectivity itself, she affirms the common assumption that the history of the notion substantively begins in the modern period. On this reading, one would not expect Aquinas to address the notion of subjectivity or related ideas such as omnisubjectivity. I disagree with this account of history; Aquinas has a notion of subjectivity, and his full account of omniscience includes most of the core desiderata of Zagzebski's characterization of omnisubjectivity.

Since the self-experience of self-love flows immediately from personal substantial unity, it is structurally prior to and grounds the possibility of further experience. In other words, personal self-experience is the subjective pole in the subject/object relation of experience and action. As a person relates to his own incommunicableness and dis-

21. Ibid., 442.
22. Ibid., 443.

tinctness in proper self-love, the experience is irreducible relative to other human beings. Each person has his own incommunicable conscious self-experience. Again, this is the difference between unity and union at the subjective level. Ontological unity entails that a thing is what it is and does not share its being with another. Each person has his own unique subjective self-experience deriving from personal unity. Thus, conscious self-experience is irreducible to another person's self-experience, and so on with every human person. Moreover, all consequent perception experience, as grounded upon and as an extension of personal self-experience, takes on the same irreducible character.

According to my interpretation of Aquinas, persons have subjectivity due to their participation in God. Due to this connection, subjectivity has the distinct characteristics it does. This link between God and human subjectivity provides the basis for how God's omniscience extends to understanding things from the first-person perspective of each human being.

Zagzebski defines omnisubjectivity as "the property of consciously grasping with perfect accuracy and completeness every conscious state of every creature from that creature's first-person perspective."[23] In Aquinas's overview of the knowledge of God, he emphasizes the intimacy of God's knowledge of creation and of human beings in particular.

> To have a proper knowledge of things is to know them not only in general, but as they are distinct from each other. Now God knows things in that manner. Hence it is written that He reaches *even to the division of the soul and the spirit, of the joints also and the marrow, and is a discerner of the thoughts and intents of the heart.*[24]

Addressing similar concerns as those Zagzebski expresses about divine intimacy, Aquinas speaks to the affinity of the notion of God with various religious practices such as prayer and forming a friend-

---

23. Zagzebski, *Omnisubjectivity*, 10.
24. *ST* I, q. 14, a. 6, *sed contra*.

ship with God. The question, though, is whether by God knowing the thoughts of a human being, Aquinas means anything like God's grasping of things from that individual's first-person perspective. To show that it is reasonable to think that Aquinas does have such an understanding, let us turn first to his analysis of omniscience and then to how the notions of participation and human subjectivity tie into his full account of God's knowledge.

Aquinas's account of omniscience begins with God's knowledge of himself. God "understands Himself through Himself."[25] Aquinas identifies God's knowledge of himself as the means by which God understands each and everything outside of himself.

> So, we say that God sees Himself in Himself, because He sees Himself through His essence; and He sees other things not in themselves, but in Himself; inasmuch as His essence contains the similitude of things other than Himself.[26]

God's essence contains the likeness and perfection of all things in virtue of the participated reality of those things, as discussed in chapter 3. In this context, the participatory relation allows God to know other things in the act of understanding his own essence.

> As therefore the essence of God contains in itself all the perfection contained in the essence of any other being, and far more, God can know in Himself all of them with proper knowledge. For the nature proper to each thing consists in some degree of participation in the divine perfection.[27]

In this way, Aquinas connects omniscience to his metaphysics of participation.

One might object that this account of God's knowledge necessarily eliminates the possibility of not only omnisubjectivity, but even of God's knowledge of any person's conscious states from that person's perspective. God knows only his own essence in a direct sense. The objection is that human subjectivity is wholly separate from God's essence. Therefore, God cannot directly know another

---

25. *ST* I, q. 14, a. 2.
26. *ST* I, q. 14, a. 5.
27. *ST* I, q. 14, a. 6.

person's first-person perspective. Perhaps he could know that persons have such experiences, but not what those experiences are like in the ways previously discussed.

I contend that Aquinas would respond to this objection by denying the second premise regarding the complete separation of human subjectivity from God's essence. On his view, human subjectivity, like everything else, does connect to God's essence by way of participation. In fact, it connects in a fundamental manner. Each person's being imitates divine goodness. God knows a person's experiences as that person experiences precisely because a person's metaphysical union with God makes possible the person's subjectivity. Again, a human being's unity has its source in God establishing a necessary relationality to himself. Thereby, in the act of understanding his own essence, God grasps both the objective and subjective aspects of creation. In short, human subjectivity is a participation in and an imitation of aspects of the divine essence. God knows each person's own perspective, since at the deepest metaphysical level, this perspective itself is a participation in God's own essence.

Aquinas goes a step further by identifying personhood as what is most perfect in all of creation. The love of self forms the basis for the activity of relating to oneself as an incommunicable person. In Aquinas's metaphysics of participation, the more perfect a thing is, the more it participates in God's essence. This is to say, in virtue of a greater participation in God, a thing possesses greater goodness and perfection. Thus, as the most perfect way of being, personhood participates in God in the most perfect manner relative to everything else in the created order. Since God has knowledge of anything through knowledge of his own essence's perfection, human personhood, the most basic activity of which is subjective self-experience, is not only knowable to God, but is supremely knowable relative to everything else.

As a unified substance, every individual person has his own participation in the divine essence distinct from or incommunicable with that of other persons. Moreover, the difference between unity and union necessitates that each person has his own unique self-experience irreducible to any other human being's self-experience. However, the same irreducibility does not pertain to God in relation to individual persons. A person's self-experience is reducible, in a real sense, to the divine essence in virtue of the metaphysics of participation—each human person fully depends upon God both for his being and associated self-experience. As discussed in chapter 3, God is existence; human beings only have existence through participation. Insofar as God experiences this difference as the subjective level, he cannot "confuse" his own experience with the experience of a created person; the latter is only a finite, derived reality.

In addition, as sinful, a human person experiences morally bad intentions and experiences immoral actions as delightful and good. One might wonder if God, by anchoring a person's self-experience, would experience either something bad as good or an evil intention. I respond by saying "yes and no." God knows Mary's immoral hatred of John from Mary's perspective, but inescapably also knows this hatred's departure from what should be present. God sees the privation that Mary might not see. In effect, God knows more, but not less, than Mary's first-person perspective. He knows as Mary knows, but simultaneously knows the deficiencies of Mary's own experience in a way she cannot.

Participation in God entails a notable difference between Zagzebski's (and most modern and contemporary accounts') and Aquinas's understanding of subjectivity. For Aquinas, human subjectivity is not irreducible as such; it is only irreducible relative to other human beings. Since only God exists necessarily and not by way of participation, only his subjectivity is irreducible per se. In spite of this key difference, Aquinas's account affirms, or at least contains the resources, to affirm the important feature discussed by Zagzebski—namely, that each person has his own first-person perspective not shared (in fact or in principle) with other human beings. Each person's experience is analogous, but never identical or reducible to another person's perspective.

SUBJECTIVITY IN LIGHT OF CHARITY

To conclude this chapter, let us look at Thomistic subjectivity in relation to God, both naturally and as transformed by charity. Aquinas's account of self-experience follows his account of being in general. The act of being is not static, but rather dynamic and relational. Due to the objective, ontological connection to the universal good within a person's being, his subjective self-experience includes an awareness of and attraction to both particular goods and universal goodness as such. To be consciously aware of one's self is to be aware of this pull toward the universal good; it colors the very nature of self-experience. If a person progresses to apprehend the universal good as God, he becomes aware of God as the center of gravity to which his conscious life is being pulled. Fully realized Thomistic subjectivity includes the ongoing experience of oneself as directed and pulled toward God.

The term of the subjective pull is the highest union with God possible. Objectively, a person strives for a union with God surpassing his very own unity with himself, due to his unity's necessary grounding in God. At the subjective level, a person desires an experiential union with God that is deeper than his ongoing self-experience. Based on Thomistic principles, such a union is possible insofar as the Holy Spirit dwells within a person, transforming his ongoing self-experience at its root. This process begins naturally with religion and culminates supernaturally in charity.

As mentioned, Aquinas holds that the quality of self-experience is proportionate to the quality of self-love. Wicked persons have "no wish to be preserved in the integrity of the inward man, nor do they desire spiritual goods for him, nor do they work for that end, nor do they take pleasure in their own company by entering into their own hearts, because whatever they find there, present, past and future is evil and horrible,"[28] whereas persons with appropriately developed self-love direct themselves "to the inward man, because they wish

---

28. *ST* II-II, q. 25, a. 7.

the preservation thereof in its integrity ... and they take pleasure in entering into their own hearts."[29]

Fostering integrity is the key principle that runs throughout Aquinas's commentary on the interconnectedness of self-love and self-experience. If a person tends toward evil, the integrity of his substantial unity is compromised, and he experiences this breach as misery. If a person tends toward good, he achieves integrity and experiences an integrated interior life with delight and peace. Due to a person's relational identity to God as established through participation, the love of God through charity serves as the ultimate integrating factor.

The reason we need this love [of charity] is because it *is the bond of perfection* ... all the virtues perfect man, but love unites them to each other and makes them permanent; and this is why it is said to bind. Or, it is said to bind because *it is the bond* of its very nature, for love unites the beloved to lover ... a thing is perfect when it holds firmly to its ultimate end; and love does this.[30]

As we have seen throughout this analysis, Aquinas frequently cites the Dionysian principle that love unites and binds. The love of God does not merely unite and bind a person to God, but also that person to himself—to his true self. When proper, the love of God and love of self in no way compete with one another. In chapter 3, we briefly considered Stump's explanation of this point of Aquinas.

On Aquinas's views, for every person, internal integration is necessary for the real good for that person, and the ultimate real good is union with God.... So, on Aquinas's account, love of oneself is in fact necessary for any love of another, including God. A perfect love of God, therefore, cannot compete with the love of oneself. A perfect love of God *requires* love of oneself.[31]

Love of God requires the love of self, but as it clear from the previous chapter, a perfect love of self requires the love of God.

---

29. Ibid.
30. Aquinas, *Commentary on the Letter of Saint Paul to the Colossians*, 163, emphasis in original.
31. Stump, *Wandering in Darkness*, 101–2.

Self-love requires the love of God because what it is to be a human person is to be already united to God by participation. Full integration depends upon more than human effort, because God, with whom a person is metaphysically related via participation, must meet the person halfway, so to speak. Insofar as personal existence includes a subjective dimension, it is fitting that fully integrated self-experience involves an experience of God, an experience that surpasses the intimacy of unions with others and oneself alone.

As friendship with God, the love of charity involves this kind of conscious union with God. In chapter 5, we looked at how some of the properties of friendship manifest themselves in divine friendship. Let us look at these properties explicitly in terms of subjectivity. Friendship is a habitual, conscious union between two persons. Aquinas contends that mutual indwelling, replete with the marks of ecstasy, conversing, sharing, trust, and fervor, demonstrates friendship's ability to effect intense unions between persons. At its limit, friendship reaches to the heart, the innermost personal core of the beloved, allowing for a shared life and even something approaching mutual experience.

Since human friendship involves the union between two substances, the nature and intensity of the union can at best closely approximate a person's own unity. To highlight this in terms from the preceding section, each person has his own self-experience with its own irreducibility. As irreducible, the two persons cannot literally merge their subjective experience into one. However, as discussed in chapter 2, the greater the objective similitude undergirding friendship is, the greater the approximation to one's unity, and the greater the affective and real unions the friendship effects. Moreover, marriage as the greatest human friendship possible involves the extension of one's self-love to the degree possible to include the beloved as a quasi-part of one's unity. Thus, in the greatest human friendship, a person will experience himself nearly in the same way that his beloved experiences him and vice versa. Aquinas makes the case that indissolubility renders such a stout approximation to substantial unity possible. A person's unique connection to God allows for an experience of even greater intimacy, depth, and continuity than occurs in marital friendship.

In virtue of a person's participation in the good, he has a metaphysical relation to God that entails that his very substantial unity necessarily relates to God. Thus, this connection allows for an intimacy with God greater than the intimacy found in any other friendship, a connection even deeper than self-experience. For Aquinas, God knows a person more than he knows himself. Also, due to this metaphysical relation, there is no physical separation between oneself as lover and God as beloved (and vice versa). The kind of friendship possible with him is one that is deeply intimate and continual. For Aquinas, charity effects this union imperfectly in this life, but perfectly in the life to come.

All of the marks of friendship manifest themselves in divine friendship, particularly the foundational mark of mutual indwelling. In this case, the Holy Spirit dwells within the heart of the person. Subjectively, a person experiences the person of the Holy Spirit both intellectually and affectively, inchoately in this life but perfectly in the next. Aquinas speaks to how God reveals his heart directly to the heart of his beloved and vice versa. Affectively, God creates the conditions within the beloved's heart to allow for delight in him.

> To get a man to the beatitude of divine enjoyment which is proper to God in His own nature, these are necessary: first, that by spiritual perfections he be likened to God; then, that he operate with these perfections; and thus, lastly, achieve that beatitude we mentioned. Of course, the spiritual gifts are given to us by the Holy Spirit.... And thus by the Holy Spirit we are configured to God and through Him we are made ready for good operation.[32]

Going into more detail, Aquinas notes that by sharing his wisdom, God reveals the secrets of his heart to the beloved.

---

32. *ScG* IV, c. 21, p. 8.

For the true sign of friendship is that a friend reveals the secrets of his heart to his friend. Since friends have one mind and heart, it does not seem that what one friend reveals to another is placed outside his own heart.... Now God reveals his secrets to us by letting us share in his wisdom.[33]

Continuing in the next chapter, Aquinas adds the following concerning the delight to be experienced in divine friendship:

Since, then, the Holy Spirit constitutes us God's friends, and makes Him dwell in us, and us dwell in Him ... it follows that through the Holy Spirit we have joy in God and security against all the world's adversities and assaults.[34]

The Holy Spirit configures the person for the experience of God through charity. This involves the activity of perfecting the experiential dimension of the love of self. Divine configuration integrates a person interiorly in the heart. "For man's perfection depends on his heart's being concentrated upon one thing; because the more a person is one, the more like unto God he is, who is truly one."[35] The greater the love of God, the greater integration of one's unity and self-love. Again, self-love becomes disordered by loving both a self that does not really exist, such as the imagined self-excellence of pride, and the wrong aspects of oneself—gravitating to the corporeal aspects at the expense of the rational. Wicked self-love produces psychic disintegration. Proper self-love produces psychic integration, and this due to the conscious union with God. Out of charity, the person exercising proper self-love wills the good to himself and experiences delight and concord with God. Most importantly, through the mutual indwelling between himself and God, he experiences God as more closely united to him than he is one with himself through his own unity.

---

33. Aquinas, *Commentary on the Gospel of John*, 2016.
34. ScG IV, c. 22, p. 3.
35. Aquinas, *Commentary on the First Letter of Saint Paul to Timothy*, trans. Fr. Fabian R. Larcher, OP, ed. J. Mortensen and E. Alarcon (Lander, Wyo.: Aquinas Institute for the Study of Sacred Doctrine, 2012), 249.

Aquinas speaks of the meaning of the kingdom of God as governed by the law of love.[36] Moreover, the extension of the kingdom of God pertains principally to the interior life rather than to external acts, though the latter are a natural expression of the former.

> [The] kingdom of God consists chiefly in internal acts: but as a consequence all things that are essential to internal acts belong to the kingdom of God. Thus, if the kingdom of God is internal righteousness, peace, and spiritual joy, all external acts that are incompatible with righteousness, peace, and spiritual joy, are in opposition to the kingdom of God.[37]

At its most perfect, union with God through charity is a self-experience thoroughly united to God. A person having united himself to God so closely—a special closeness made possible by the underlying metaphysical connection of participation—experiences himself as rooted in God.

In a God-centered love of self, a person's ongoing self-experience is one of integration and the peace that issues from the tranquility of order. This serves to strengthen the bonds between persons in friendship. Using marriage as the prime example, since it is the greatest human friendship, it allows for the greatest union and greatest possible shared experience between human beings. If each spouse's self-experience is perfected through a friendship with God, that self-experience will be integrated, pleasant, and peaceful. Moreover, since Aquinas characterizes personal identity in this relational way—namely, the relation of the human person to God—each spouse will be related to the same thing. This relation is not just an objective relation; it is subjectively experienced on the basis of love. Each person's self-experience will remain irreducible, but as each person's self-experience is rooted in the same ultimate source—namely, God—the commonality between them will be as great as possible. Thus, the shared experience of union between them will approximate as closely as metaphysically possible to unity, and so on to lesser degrees in unions with others persons in friendship.

---

36. *ST* I-II, q. 107, a. 1, ad 2.
37. *ST* I-II, q. 108, a. 1, ad 1.

The Love of Self and Subjectivity

To summarize this chapter, since union derives from unity, and thus the experience of others in friendship derives from the ways a person relates to himself in the love of self, Aquinas's account of self-love includes a dimension of subjective self-experience. The experience of oneself through self-love precedes the experience of others in the love of friendship and contains the sources of all the properties of the latter. Since the love of self proceeds immediately from substantial unity and personal substantial unity is unique and incommunicable, the self-experience caused by self-love is unique or irreducible to the analogous self-experience of others. Finally, because of unity's roots in God by way of metaphysical participation, the self-experience of self-love tends toward God, finding its full perfection and integration in a conscious union of friendship with him.

Conclusion

In the *Nicomachean Ethics*, Aristotle notes that all people agree that they want happiness. Once the question arises concerning what happiness is, people no longer agree and offer varied and incompatible notions of the nature of happiness. Similarly, it is safe to assert that most people agree that love is essential, if not absolutely central, to a meaningful human life. Nonetheless, when one asks the next logical question of what love is, the agreement dissipates into a myriad of views. Perhaps more unfortunately, assuming that love does indeed constitute a central element to a meaningful human existence, most people, when reflecting on how well they love and receive love (whatever their view of its nature may be), are not satisfied with their efforts toward being loving persons.

For Aquinas, love, both in terms of the act of willing the good and the real union it effects, is the key to genuine, sustainable joy and, by extension, to a meaningful, flourishing human existence. While of ultimate importance, love is not freestanding; it rests upon and is structured by underlying metaphysical facts. The unity of substantial oneness determines a priority of the love of self over the love of others. Moreover, the ways in which a person relates to himself in the love of self serves as the guiding principle for how he relates to others. The unity of substantial oneness, in turn, is what it is through participation in God. A person cannot love himself properly without loving God properly, which in this case entails loving God more than self.

Conclusion

As these metaphysical relations establish the contours of human flourishing, a person secures a good life by loving in the right ways while avoiding improper love—particularly improper love of self. Each person has a proper moral space and duty to govern and direct his own life. However, Aquinas cautions against any form of autonomy based on selfishness. To govern oneself selfishly is to attempt to create an identity that is fundamentally nonrelational. Such self-preoccupation, as running contrary to the natural orientation of self-love, will ultimately culminate in a spiteful or slothful self-isolation (or both). Loving self-governance requires the elimination of a prideful self-will and the promotion of submission to the good.

If the general thrust of Aquinas's account of love is correct, both in terms of the nature of love as willing the good and the structure of being as determining the proper order of love, it could go a long way in providing a couple of practical suggestions on how to love. First, love as an act of the will has important implications. Love does not just happen. A person chooses to love, and if he does not choose to love, love will not occur. Of course, choosing to love does not guarantee others will love him, but it certainly raises the probability of reciprocation. Second, the priority of the love of self over the love of others has its own implications. Loving other human beings is the last step, so to speak, in the order of love. Thus, to love well, a person must give priority to cultivating the love of self through the virtues. Sustainable joy and real concord with others depend upon these virtues. Consequently, cultivating the virtues is a practical necessity to long-term friendships that offer real delight and concord.

Perhaps the objection will be raised that, even if love as an act of the will is part of what makes love love, there is more to it than that. For instance, love as an act of the will does not seem to account adequately for the immediate connections that sometimes arise in love, particularly in the context of romantic love. Aquinas would agree with this objection and point to his full account of love involving three unions. The union of similitude makes love as the union of affection possible. Sometimes the similitude between two persons will facilitate an immediate attraction. More importantly, the union of affection is exactly that: it is a feeling state inclining the will toward the goodness of the other, but for love to become actual or fully realized, the person must choose to will the good to the other for the sake of the other. Again, this leads to the union of possession or the real union between them, replete with mutual indwelling and all the other marks previously addressed.

These three unions are part of complete, perfect love. Aquinas realizes that life is imperfect. A person may not always have the full affective complacency toward the other person, but the will as will can still choose the good on behalf of the other. To promote an affective complacency toward the other person consistently over the long term, Aquinas again points to the necessary role of the virtues. The more a person cultivates the will through justice and religion, and supernaturally through charity (and the other powers through their respective virtues), the more well-ordered his love will be, and the more desirable affectivity he will experience, both in terms of longing for the beloved as well as in terms of experiencing the joy of being with the beloved.

To conclude this book, let us turn to two other virtues Aquinas considers to be absolutely essential to the perfection of the love of self and thus to a life of love of and joy: namely, humility and magnanimity. Humility perfects the will by restraining it from the tendency toward self-exaltation and the construction of a nonrelational identity. In other words, humility directly opposes the prideful self-love and thus cuts off the problems created by the latter at their source. Part of understanding what Aquinas means by humility requires grasping what humility is not. In this case, humility is not fainteartedness or pusillanimity. In fact, Aquinas explicitly treats the latter as a vice, a disposition inclining one to shrink from the demands of love.

Humility stands with the virtue of magnanimity at the heart of human activity. To be humble is not to be of weak or small spirit, but rather to be bold, fervent, and strong in one's love.

The difficult good has something attractive to the appetite, namely the aspect of good, and likewise something repulsive to the appetite, namely the difficulty of obtaining it. In respect to the former there arises the movement of hope, and in respect to the latter, the movement of despair ... for those appetitive movements which are a kind of impulse toward an object, there is need of a moderating and restraining moral virtue, while for those which are a kind of recoil, there is need, on the part of the appetite, of a moral virtue to strengthen it and urge it on. Wherefore a twofold virtue is necessary with regard to the difficult good: one, to temper and restrain the mind, lest it tend to things immoderately; and this belongs to the virtue of humility: and another to strengthen the mind against despair, and urge it on to the pursuit of great things according to right reason; and this is magnanimity.[1]

Pursuing a life focused on proper love—a lifelong pursuit of proper goods both for oneself and for others—is not easy; it requires discipline, vigilance, and strength.

Humility is essential for love to combat a selfishness of the will. Without humility, the love of self becomes improper by favoring oneself in an exaggerated fashion. Again, this frustrates the double relational identity of a person as related to God by participation and is related to others as unity naturally inclines one to union with others. Love without humility can end in a bitter loneliness. Love nurtured by humility eschews selfishness in favor of self-giving and union.

Insofar as seeking real goods for oneself and others can be difficult, the will (and sense appetites) must be strengthened by magnanimity, urging a person to do those things of which he is capable. Aquinas characterizes the great-souled person, like he does with every virtue, in terms of the measure of love. A magnanimous person wills and acquires true goods to oneself even when inconvenient or painful. Insofar as the magnanimous person relates to others as he does himself, he also wills and acquires goods for others, even when inconvenient or painful. Magnanimity steels a person's will for the tasks of willing the good for the sake of the other, even in those mo-

---

1. *ST* II-II, q. 161, a. 1.

ments where the affections might fall silent while the requirements of love remain the same.

In short, love is a choice, but loving rightly in a consistent manner is not easy. Without the full range of moral virtues cultivating practical reason, the appetites, and the will, a life of proper love cannot be had. Nonetheless, for Aquinas, the metaphysical facts of human existence establish that a life of deep joy and fulfillment can only come through proper love: first, the love of God; second, the love of self; third, the love of others. Thus, whatever the difficulties, a life of love is worth the effort.

Bibliography

Aquinas, Thomas. *Commentary on Aristotle's Nicomachean Ethics*. Translated by C. I. Litzinger, OP. Notre Dame: Ind.: Dumb Ox, 1993.

———. *Commentary on the First Letter of Saint Paul to the Corinthians*. Translated by Fr. Fabian R. Larcher, OP, B. Mortensen, and D. Keating, edited by J Mortensen and E. Alarcon. Lander, Wyo.: Aquinas Institute for the Study of Sacred Doctrine, 2012.

———. *Commentary on the First Letter of Saint Paul to Timothy*. Translated by Fr. Fabian R. Larcher, OP, edited by J. Mortensen and E. Alarcon. Lander, Wyo.: Aquinas Institute for the Study of Sacred Doctrine, 2012.

———. *Commentary on the Gospel of John*. Translated by Fr. Fabian R. Larcher, OP, edited by The Aquinas Institute. Lander, Wyo.: Aquinas Institute for the Study of Sacred Doctrine, 2013.

———. *Commentary on the Gospel of Matthew*. Translated by Jeremy Holmes and Beth Mortensen, edited by Aquinas Institute. Lander, Wyo.: Aquinas Institute for the Study of Sacred Doctrine, 2013.

———. *Commentary on the Letters of Saint Paul to the Colossians*. Translated by Fr. Fabian R. Larcher, OP, edited by J. Mortensen and E. Alarcon. Lander, Wyo.: Aquinas Institute for the Study of Sacred Doctrine, 2012.

———. *Commentary on the Letters of Saint Paul to the Galatians*. Translated by Fr. Fabian R. Larcher, OP, and M. L. Lamb, edited by J. Mortensen and E. Alarcon. Lander, Wyo.: Aquinas Institute for the Study of Sacred Doctrine, 2012.

———. *De Malo*. Vol. 23. Rome: Leonine edition, 1982.

———. *De Veritate*. Vol. 22. Rome: Leonine edition, 1970–76.

———. *Disputed Questions on Virtue*. Translated by Ralph McInerny. South Bend, Ind.: St. Augustine's Press, 1998.

———. *The Exposition of the "On the Hebdomads" of Boethius*. Translated by Janice L. Schultz and Edward A. Synan. Washington, D.C.: The Catholic University of America Press, 2001.

———. *Expositio super Iob ad litteram*. Vol. 26. Rome: Leonine edition, 1965.
———. *The Literal Exposition on Job: A Scriptural Commentary Concerning Providence*. Translated by Anthony Damico, with an interpretative essay and notes by Martin D. Yaffe. Atlanta, Ga.: Scholar's Press, 1989.
———. *On Charity*. Translated by Lottie H. Kendzierski. Milwaukee: Marquette University Press, 1984.
———. *On Evil*. Translated by Richard Regan. Oxford: Oxford University Press, 2003.
———. *On the Power of God*. Translated by the English Dominican Fathers. Westminster, Md.: Newman Press, 1952.
———. *On Truth*. Translated by James V. McGlynn, SJ, Robert W. Mulligan, SJ, and Robert W. Schmidt, SJ. Indianapolis, Ind.: Hackett, 1994.
———. *Quaestiones disputatae de potentia*. Taurini: Marietti, 1953.
———. *Quodlibetal Questions 1 and 2*. Translated by Sandra Edwards. Toronto: Pontifical Institute of Medieval Studies, 1983.
———. *Scriptum super libros Sententiarum Petri Lombardi*. From *On Love and Charity: Readings from the "Commentary on the Sentences of Peter Lombard."* Selected and translated by Peter Kwasniewki, Thomas Bolin, OSB, and Joseph Bolin. Washington, D.C: The Catholic University of America Press, 2008.
———. *Sententia libri Ethicorum*. Vol. 47. Rome: Leonine edition, 1969.
———. *Summa contra gentiles*. Vols. 13–15. Rome: Leonine edition, 1918–30.
———. *Summa contra Gentiles*. Translated by James F. Anderson, Vernon J. Bourke, Charles J. O'Neil, and Anton C. Pegis, FRSC. Notre Dame, Ind.: University of Notre Dame Press, 1975.
———. *Summa Theologica*. Translated by the Fathers of the English Dominican Province. Allen, Tex.: Christian Classics, 1981.
———. *Summa theologiae*. Vols. 4–12. Rome: Leonine edition, 1888–1906.
———. *Super Epistolam B. Pauli ad Colossenses lectura*. Taurini: Marietti, 1953.
———. *Super Epistolam B. Pauli ad Galatas lectura*. Taurini: Marietti, 1953.
———. *Super I Epistolam B. Pauli ad Corinthios lectura*. Taurini: Marietti, 1953.
———. *Super I Epistolam B. Pauli ad Timotheum lectura*. Taurini: Marietti, 1953.
———. *Super Evangelium S. Ioannis lectura*. Taurini: Marietti, 1972.
———. *Super Evangelium S. Matthaei lectura*. Taurini: Marietti, 1951.
Aristotle. *Nicomachean Ethics*. 2nd ed. Translated by Terence Irwin. Indianapolis, Ind.: Hackett, 1999.
Bobik, Joseph. "Aquinas on *Communicatio*: The Foundation of Friendship and *Caritas*." *Modern Schoolman* 64 (1986): 1–18.
Clarke, Norris, SJ. *Person and Being*. Milwaukee: Marquette University Press, 1993.
Cornish, Paul. "John Courtney Murray and St. Thomas Aquinas on Obedience and the Civil Conversation." *Vera Lex* 9, nos. 1–2 (2008): 49–75.
Cory, Therese Scarpelli. *Aquinas on Human Self-Knowledge*. Cambridge: Cambridge University Press, 2014.

Crosby, John. *The Selfhood of the Human Person*. Washington, D.C.: The Catholic University of America Press, 1996.
DeYoung, Rebecca Konyndyk. "Resistance to the Demands of Love: Aquinas on the Vice of Acedia." *Thomist* 68, no. 2 (2004): 173–204.
———. "Aquinas on the Vice of Sloth: Three Interpretive Issues." *Thomist* 75, no. 1 (2011): 43–64.
———. "Sloth: Some Historical Reflections on Laziness, Effort, and the Resistance to the Demands of Love." In *Virtues and Their Vices*, edited by Kevin Timpe and Craig A. Boyd, 177–98. Oxford: Oxford University Press, 2014.
Di Blasi, Fulvio. "Knowledge of the Good as Participation in God's Love," *Giornale di Metafisica* 27, no. 2 (2005): 469–89.
———. *God and the Natural Law: A Rereading of Thomas Aquinas*. Translated by David Thunder. South Bend, Ind.: St. Augustine's Press, 2006.
Flood, Anthony T. *The Root of Friendship: Self-Love and Self-Governance in Aquinas*. Washington, D.C.: The Catholic University of America Press, 2014.
———. "Marriage as Friendship: Aquinas's View in Light of His Account of Self-Love." *Nova et Vetera* 13, no. 2 (2015): 441–58.
———. "Aquinas on Self-Love and Love of God: The Foundations for and Perfection of Subjectivity." *International Philosophical Quarterly* 56, no. 1 (2016): 45–55.
———. "The Destructiveness of Lust and Its Cure: Reflections on Dante, Aquinas, and Wojtyla." In *Woman as Prophet in the Home and the World*, edited by R. Mary Hayden Lemmons, 163–76. Lanham, Md.: Lexington, 2016.
Gallagher, David A. "The Desire for Beatitude and the Love of Friendship in Thomas Aquinas." *Mediaeval Studies* 58 (1996): 1–47.
———. "Thomas Aquinas on Self-Love as the Basis for Love of Others." *Acta Philosophica* 8, no. 1 (1999): 23–44.
Gilson, Étienne. *The Spirit of Mediaeval Philosophy*. Notre Dame, Ind.: University of Notre Dame Press, 1991.
Krom, Michael P. "Civic Virtue: Aquinas on Piety, Observance, and Religion." *Proceedings of the American Catholic Philosophical Association* 88 (2015): 145–53.
Kwasniewski, Peter. "St. Thomas on the Grandeur and Limitations of Marriage." *Nova et Vetera* 10, no. 2 (2012): 415–36.
Lee, Patrick. "St. Thomas on Love of Self and Love of Others." In *The Renewal of Civilization: Essays in Honor of Jacques Maritain*, edited by Gavin T. Colvert, 235–52. Washington, D.C.: The Catholic University of America Press, 2010.
Lemmons, Rose Mary Hayden. *Ultimate Normative Foundations: The Case for Aquinas's Personalist Natural Law*. Lanham, Md.: Lexington, 2011.
Malloy, Christopher J. "Thomas on the Order of Love and Desire." *Thomist* 71, no. 1 (2007): 65–87.
McCluskey, Colleen. "An Unequal Relationship between Equals: Thomas Aquinas on Marriage." *History of Philosophy Quarterly* 24, no. 1 (January 2007): 1–18.

O'Reilly, Kevin, OP. "The Significance of Worship in the Thought of Thomas Aquinas: Some Reflections." *International Philosophical Quarterly* 53, no. 4 (2013): 453–62.
Osborne, Thomas M. Jr. *The Love of Self and the Love of God in Thirteenth-Century Ethics*. Notre Dame, Ind.: University of Notre Dame Press, 2005.
Pieper, Josef. *In Tune with the World: A Theory of Festivity*. Translated by Richard Winston and Clara Winston. South Bend, Ind.: St. Augustine's Press, 1999.
Porter, Jean. "Natural Equality: Freedom, Authority, and Obedience in Two Medieval Thinkers." *Annual of the Society of Christian Ethics* 21 (2001): 275–99.
Rziha, John. *Perfecting Human Actions: St. Thomas Aquinas on Human Participation in Eternal Law*. Washington, D.C: The Catholic University of America Press, 2009.
Schneewind, Jerome B. *The Invention of Autonomy*. Cambridge: Cambridge University Press, 1998.
Schwartz, Daniel. *Aquinas on Friendship*. Oxford: Oxford University Press, 2007.
Sherwin, Michael, OP. *By Knowledge and by Love: Charity and Knowledge in the Moral Theology of St. Thomas Aquinas*. Washington, D.C: The Catholic University Press of America Press, 2005.
Spencer, Mark K. "Aristotelian Substance and Personalistic Subjectivity." *International Philosophical Quarterly* 55, no. 2 (2015): 145–64.
Stump, Eleonore. *Aquinas*. London and New York: Routledge, 2003.
———. *Wandering in Darkness: Narrative and the Problem of Suffering*. Oxford: Oxford University Press, 2010.
Taylor, Charles. *Sources of the Self: The Making of the Modern Identity*. Cambridge, Mass: Harvard University Press, 1989.
———. *A Secular Age*. Cambridge, Mass.: Belknap Press of Harvard University Press, 2007.
Torrell, Jean-Pierre, OP. *Saint Thomas Aquinas*. Vol. 1, *The Person and His Work*. Translated by Robert Royal. Washington, D.C.: The Catholic University of America Press, 1996.
———. "Life and Works." In *The Oxford Handbook of Aquinas*, edited by Brian Davies and Eleonore Stump, 15–32. Oxford: Oxford University Press, 2012.
Waldstein, Michael. "John Paul II and St. Thomas on Love and the Trinity (first and second part)." *Anthropotes* 18 (2002): 113–38 and 269–86.
Wippel, John. *The Metaphysical Thought of Thomas Aquinas: From Finite Being to Uncreated Being*. Washington, D.C.: The Catholic University of America Press, 2000.
Wojtyla, Karol. "Subjectivity and the Irreducible in the Human Being." In *Person and Community: Selected Essays*, translated by Theresa Sandok, OSM, 209–17. New York: Peter Lang, 1993.
Zagzebski, Linda Trinkaus. "The Uniqueness of Persons." *Journal of Religious Ethics* 29, no. 3 (2001): 401–23.

———. "Ethical and Epistemic Egoism and the Ideal of Autonomy." *Episteme: A Journal of Social Epistemology* 4, no. 3 (2007): 252–63.

———. *Epistemic Authority: A Theory of Trust, Authority, and Autonomy in Belief.* Oxford: Oxford University Press, 2012.

———. *Omnisubjectivity: A Defense of a Divine Attribute.* Milwaukee.: Marquette University Press, 2013.

———. "Omnisubjectivity: Why It Is a Divine Attribute." *Nova et Vetera,* English Edition, 14, no. 2 (2016): 435–50.

Index

anger, 75, 79, 96
Aquinas, Thomas: charity in, 26; communication in, 10; concord in, 10–11; conformity to divine will in, 98–99; covetousness in, 73; delight in, 9–10; friendship in, 4–5, 8–11, 27–28, 129–30; hatred in, 79–80; heart in, 113–14; joy in, 10; love in, xi–xii, 9–10; love of God in, xi–xii, 45–47, 56–57; love of self in, 11–24; marriage in, 35–43; personhood in, 114–15; providence in, 60; Satan in, 81; self-governance in, 86–88; similitude in, 25; sin in, 73–77; sloth in, 77; subjectivity in, 112–13, 125; union of similitude in, 3–4; women in, 28–29, 36n11
Aquinas on Human Self-Knowledge (Cory), 112
Aristotle, 4–5, 10, 16n27, 88–89, 134
autonomy, 86–87, 135

beatitude, 14, 26, 51, 53, 87–88, 130
beneficence, 6, 11, 17–18, 23, 30, 39, 59–62, 86–88, 104, 108, 116–19
benevolence, 6, 8–11, 17–18, 23, 30–31, 39, 59–62, 86–88, 104, 108, 116–19

charity, 26, 32–34, 44, 58–62, 65, 103–4, 107–8, 127–32
children, 28–32, 35, 37, 40
Clarke, Norris, 112n4
commandments, 94, 100, 103, 104n27, 106

Commentary on I Corinthians (Aquinas), 53–54
Commentary on Galatians (Aquinas), 20, 28, 33
Commentary on John (Aquinas), 41, 108
Commentary on Matthew (Aquinas), 87–88
Commentary on the Gospel of John (Aquinas), 104n27
Commentary on the Nicomachean Ethics (Aquinas), 88
Commentary on the Sentences of Peter Lombard (Aquinas), 17
communication, 10, 39, 41–42, 56–57, 63–64, 95
concord, 10–11, 31, 33, 39, 65–66, 91, 117
concupiscence, love of, 2–4, 11, 14, 21, 32, 41–43, 51, 63, 90
conformity: action and, 97–98; devotion and, 95; to divine will, 98–99; love of God and, 71, 99; necessity of, 67–71; sin and, 67–84; union and, 68–69; will and, 109
conscience, 89, 102
conscious self-experience, 110–33
contemplation, 63–64, 95
Cory, Therese Scarpelli, 112, 118
covetousness, 73–74

Dante, 73
De Divinis Nominbus (Aquinas), 46

Index

delight, 9–11, 18, 31, 39, 65, 68, 119, 128, 130–31, 135
De Malo (Aquinas), 73
demonic temptation, 81
De Veritate (Aquinas), 22
devotion, 53, 94–95, 105
DeYoung, Rebecca Konyndyk, 76–77
Disputed Question on Charity (Aquinas), 26

ecstasy, 9, 11, 39, 41, 59, 63–65, 71, 90, 129
empathy, 122
envy, 72, 74–75, 78, 96
eudaimonism, 85–86

family, 28–31, 35, 37, 40
fear, 105–7
festivity, 92–93
friendship: in Aquinas, 4–5, 8–11, 27–28, 129–30; charity and, 33, 44; by choice, 27; communication and, 10; concord and, 10–11, 31; intensity and, 39–40; joy and, 10; longing and, 17–18; love of, 6–7; love of God and, 53–54, 56, 130–31; and love of self, xii, 16–17, 116–17, 131; marriage as, xiv, 36–39; and mutual indwelling, 7–8; of natural origin, 27–28, 30; obedience and, 104–5; personal presence and, 8–9; personhood and, 6–7; of pleasure, 4; propinquity and, 8–9; self-governance and, 91; selfishness and, 88–89; subjectivity and, 116–18; true, 4–6; union and, 1–11, 129; and union of similitude, 5–6; of utility, 4

Gallagher, David, 14, 46
Gilson, Étienne, 49
gluttony, 73, 78, 90
grace, 19–20, 32, 45, 47–49, 53–54, 58–59, 108
greed, 73, 78, 90
Gregory the Great, 73

happiness, 57, 87–88, 134
hatred, 43, 71–80, 82, 94, 106, 126
heart, 7, 113–15
Holy Spirit, 57, 63, 105–6, 130
humility, 136–37

integrity, 17n18, 117, 127–28
In Tune with the World (Pieper), 92

Job, 81, 83
joy, 10, 20, 22, 28, 34, 52–53, 58, 65, 90–94, 101, 136
justice, 22, 34, 52–53, 91, 101–2

kingdom of God, 132

law, 60, 72, 83–84, 88, 99–100, 102, 106, 109, 132
Lemmons, Rose Mary Hayden, 28n3
longing, 8, 11, 17, 30, 39, 59, 63–64, 116, 119, 136
love: in Aquinas, xi–xii, 9–10; of concupiscence, 2–4, 11, 14, 21, 32, 41–43, 51, 63, 90; delight and, 9–10; ecstasy and, 9; effects of, 9; of friendship, 6–7; and obedience to divine will, 97–109; object of, 26, 33; personal presence and, 8–9; self-governance and, 85–91; worship and, 91–97
love of God: in Aquinas, xi–xii, 45–47, 56–57; charity and, 33, 44, 58–59, 61–62; communication and, 56–57, 63–64; concord and, 65–66; conformity and, 71, 99; contemplation and, 64; friendship and, 53–54, 56, 130–31; vs. love of others, 48; and love of self, 44–50, 54–55, 69, 108–9, 128–29; natural inclination to, 50–56; natural principles and, 54; participation and, 44–66; providence and, 59–61; prudence and, 60–61; sin and, 82–83; sloth and, 94–95; supernatural, 56–66; union and, 44–45
love of self: in Aquinas, 11–24; charity and, 34, 108; and conscious self-experience, 110–33; cultivation and, 90–91; disordered, 69–71; friendship and, xii, 16–17, 116–17, 131; and gift of self, 42–43; God-centered, 132; humility and, 137; justice and, 22; and love between parents and children, 31–32; and love of God, 44–50, 54–55, 69, 108–9, 128–29; and love of others, 22–23; marriage and, 36, 40–43; pride and, 70; sacrifice and, 96; self-experience and, 117–18;

self-governance and, 86–87; selfishness and, 18–19, 21n32; sin and, 69–72, 79–80, 82; sloth and, 78; and subjectivity, 110–33; subjectivity and, 113, 127–28; union and, 3, 12–13, 92, 107, 115–16, 118–19; will in, 13–16, 119
lust, 73–74, 78, 90

magnanimity, 136–38
Malloy, Christopher, 3n2
marriage, xiv, 25, 28, 30, 35–43, 59, 129, 132
McCluskey, Colleen, 36n11
melting, 9, 59, 63–65
moral precepts, 100
mutual indwelling, 7–9, 11, 13, 39, 43, 54, 59, 63–65, 82, 90, 107, 118, 129–31, 136

Nicomachean Ethics (Aristotle), 134

oaths, 94–97
obedience to divine will, 97–109
observance, 53n23
omniscience, 120–22, 124
omnisubjectivity, 120–26
Osborne, Thomas, 47

parents, 28–32, 35, 37, 40
participation, 44–66, 108–9, 120–26
personal presence, 8–9
personhood, 6–7, 114–15, 125–26
Pieper, Joseph, 92–94, 96
piety, 53–54, 63
Porter, Jean, 103n24
possession, union of, xiii, 3–4, 7, 12, 25–32, 39–40, 68, 100, 115–16, 136
prayer, 53, 92, 94–96, 105, 121, 123
presence, personal, 8–9
pride, 16, 22, 65, 70–75, 78–80, 97, 131, 135–36
propinquity, 8–9
providence, 59–61, 83–84
prudence, 60–61, 101–2
Purgatorio (Dante), 73

Quodlibet (Aquinas), 49

religion, 52–54, 91–97, 104–5

sacrifice, 92–94, 96
Satan, 80–84
Schneewind, Jerome B., 101n20
self, love of. *See* love of self
self-experience, 110–33
self-governance, 62, 85–91, 103, 106–7
selfishness, 18–19, 21n32, 34, 88–89, 135
similitude, union of, 3–4, 5–6, 12, 19, 24–35, 37, 39, 46, 48, 55, 57, 108, 117, 135–36
sin(s): in Aquinas, 73–77; charity and, 34, 58; conformity and, 67–84; defined, 71; hatred and, 71–80; love of God and, 82–83; love of self and, 69–72, 79–80, 82; marriage and, 37; natural love and, 32; pride and, 70; seven deadly, 72–73; severity of, 74. *See also specific sins*
sloth, 76–78, 94–95
Spencer, Mark K., 113n7
Stump, Eleonore, 8–9, 22–23, 128
subjectivity: in Aquinas, 112–13, 125; charity and, 127–32; as conscious self-experience, 110–11; empathy and, 122; experiential, 111–12; friendship and, 116–18; interior, 111–12; irreducible, 111–12, 119–26; and love of self, 127–28; love of self and, 110–33; omnisubjectivity, 120–26; participation and, 120–26; personhood and, 125–26; union and, 127
Summa contra Gentiles (Aquinas), 7, 36
Summa Theologiae (Aquinas), 2, 7–8, 26, 45n4, 73
sustainability, 32, 67, 85–86, 90–91, 134–35

Taylor, Charles, 111
temptation, 70, 80–84

union: conformity and, 68–69; degrees of, 25–43; friendship and, 1–11, 129; and love of concupiscence, 2–3; and love of God, 44–45, 48; and love of self, 3, 12–13, 92, 107, 115–16, 118–19; marriage as, 35–43; metaphysics of, 4; of possession, xiii, 3–4, 7, 12, 25–32, 39–40, 68, 100, 115–16, 136; self-governance and, 87; of similitude, 3–6, 12, 19, 24–35, 37, 39, 46, 48, 55, 57, 108, 117, 135–36; subjectivity and, 127; unity and, 11, 35; from unity to, 18–28; unity vs., 123

unity: and love of self, 11–18, 39; marriage and, 38, 42; to union, 18–28; union and, 11, 35; union vs., 123

vainglory, 73–75, 102
vice, 54–55, 79. See also sin(s); and specific vices

Waldstein, Michael, 41–42
will: conformity and, 109; love as act of, 135; in love of self, 13–16, 119; magnanimity and, 137–38; obedience to divine, 97–109; and self-knowledge, 118
Wippel, John, 49
Wojtyla, Karol, 41, 110–11, 114n11
women, 28–29, 36n11
worship, 53, 91–97
wrath, 75. See also anger

Zagzebski, Linda Trinkaus, 7n8, 19n30, 111, 120–23

ALSO IN THE
THOMISTIC RESSOURCEMENT SERIES

———————:———————

Series Editors: Matthew Levering
Thomas Joseph White, OP

The Cleansing of the Heart
The Sacraments as Instrumental Causes in the Thomistic Tradition
Reginald M. Lynch, OP

The Ideal Bishop
Aquinas's Commentaries on the Pastoral Epistles
Michael G. Sirilla

Aquinas and the Theology of the Body
The Thomistic Foundations of John Paul II's Anthropology
Thomas Petri, OP

Angels and Demons
A Catholic Introduction
Serge-Thomas Bonino, OP
Translated by Michael J. Miller

The Incarnate Lord
A Thomistic Study in Christology
Thomas Joseph White, OP

The Mystery of Union with God
Dionysian Mysticism in Albert the Great and Thomas Aquinas
Bernhard Blankenhorn, OP

www.ingramcontent.com/pod-product-compliance
Lightning Source LLC
Chambersburg PA
CBHW070257010526
44107CB00056B/2482